GRACE

THE MOST UNDERUTILIZED STRENGTH IN BUSINESS

A LEADERSHIP FABLE

BY

CALVIN D. MORRIS

TABLE OF CONTENTS

For Jacqueline

"If your actions inspire others to dream more, learn more, do more and become more, you are a leader."

— John Quincy Adams

INTRODUCTION

Very few leaders, coaches, teams, organizations—understand the true power of grace. My friend, the CEO of a Fortune 500 company, once said, "Grace is the glue that holds organizations together; not meetings, not trust falls, not potlucks, not bonuses, not incentives, but grace. No organization can sustain without it. Those that have it," he explained, "survive longer than those that don't."

Whenever I share this perspective with leaders, particularly those grappling with struggling organizations, they immediately seek my definition of grace. Not because they doubt its value, but because, to them, grace feels too abstract, too metaphysical to carry real strategic weight. The sticking point, they explain is its intangible nature, which limits its influence on action, policy, or performance.

While this perception may seem innocuous, it can have serious repercussions. Leaders who dismiss grace as vague often remain stuck, watching opportunities slip away, while those who embrace it move forward, creating space for adaptation, evolution, and growth.

During times of declining sales, low foot traffic, and mounting complaints, the stark contrast between these two types of leaders becomes evident. One group clings to fear, blame, and control, while the other embraces trust, collaboration, and renewal. In this divide, the presence or absence of grace profoundly influences every interaction, decision, and outcome. Grace, the most underutilized strength in business, becomes paramount when pressure reaches its peak. Leaders who take it for granted often create conditions that foster five critical patterns.

To illustrate how these patterns manifest, this book presents a narrative. Within its pages, you'll encounter Janis Harbinger, a visual mathematician who employed grace to salvage a struggling company. In her desperate quest for answers, she stumbles upon five patterns that are prevalent in every struggling retail store. These patterns are undeniable, yet even well-intentioned leaders find it challenging to confront them, as doing so can feel like acknowledging personal failure.

This story serves as merely the beginning. To facilitate the application of its lessons, the book also includes a comprehensive set of practical resources in the back: worksheets, assessments, and tools meticulously designed to cater to your team's unique challenges.

Following these resources lies a deeper exploration of the five patterns, accompanied by practical guidance on navigating the real-world challenges they present. Each section delves into the reasons behind their emergence, their root causes, and the strategies required to overcome them. Whether you're leading a small team or managing a large operation, these insights are intended to transcend mere awareness and catalyze meaningful, lasting action.

Ultimately, if you and your team collaborate effectively, you can eliminate the five patterns and uncover something far more potent: the true potential of grace.

THE FABLE BEGINS

PART ONE:

THE FALL FROM GRACE

SHOCK

Shock occurs when Plan A turns into Plan B,
Plan B morphs into Plan C, and Plan C starts looking
like no plan at all.

The retail giant QB-KOZE was undeniably in shock
and ZinkaTech was only one bad decision away from
joining it.

THE DECISION

From its launch in Farmington Hills, ZinkaTech appeared unstoppable. It boasted buzz, funding, talent, and momentum. Nominated Start-Up of the Year, it was celebrated as an ideal workplace for aspiring entrepreneurs and widely praised on social platforms. ZinkaTech quickly expanded as investors poured in from across the globe. In just two years, it transitioned from tech and business services to its own line of business products.

Flush with confidence and capital, the leadership team set its sights on retail. That's when they acquired QB-KOZE, a well-known office supply chain with locations across the Midwest. On paper, the move seemed brilliant—a swift and strategic entry into a mature market, complete with an established customer base and physical infrastructure. However, while the numbers appeared strong, the human side of the business revealed a very different story.

Beneath the surface, QB-KOZE was already in serious trouble. Its culture was deeply fractured. Its leadership team was combative, and employee morale was dangerously low. Resistance to change wasn't just present; it had become ingrained in the company's DNA. Despite its optimism, ZinkaTech was unprepared for what it had inherited.

The cracks began to show almost immediately. ZinkaTech's leaders attempted various approaches to bridge the gaps, but their efforts were inconsistent and poorly aligned. These were classic signs of shock. One month brought stricter rules, while the next month brought sudden leniency. However, the deeper issue wasn't strategy; it was confidence.

As results faltered, the leadership team began to doubt themselves. The clarity that fueled their early success dissolved into hesitation, confusion, and conflict. Leaders who had once inspired began to second-guess. Worse, they started to lose faith in their teams.

Morale plummeted. Employees were expected to embrace change swiftly, yet little compassion was shown to those struggling. Support was scarce, appearing only when leaders needed to showcase positive results in engagement surveys. Fear infiltrated decision-making, causing hesitation and uncertainty among employees. They questioned who to trust and which direction to take.

Sales then plummeted, leading to key managers' resignations. Disillusioned employees vented their frustrations online, portraying the company as disorganized, dismissive, and unstable. The brand's reputation suffered a significant blow. The pressure on the CEO intensified until he was ultimately removed.

Leaderless, ZinkaTech spiraled into disarray. Political maneuvering replaced strategic planning, causing product launches to stall. Investors withdrew, and stores shuttered. The final blow came with a major data breach that exposed customer information and shattered the remaining trust. Desperate for help, the board reached out to Brad, who promptly contacted Janis.

JANIS HARBINGER

Her husband, a companion, friend, mentor, and rock, passed away just seven months after his diagnosis of pancreatic cancer. Janis loved him deeply and admired his ability to always know what to do, which grounded her and made life seem meaningful. Without him, she felt lost, alone, and exposed.

The first month after his passing was the hardest. Grief overwhelmed her, leaving her numb and untethered. She shut herself in the house, as if the world outside had ceased to exist. Her routines dissolved, and she stopped caring about appearances, dying her blonde hair a muted autumn brown and letting the polish chip from her nails. Even the smallest decisions felt too heavy to make.

Then came the bills. To her surprise, she struggled financially. Jacob had always handled the money, and though he'd been meticulous, he never shared the details of his system. Now, without instructions or access codes, Janis was left trying to piece together a life that had been carefully maintained by someone who was no longer there. The constant ringing of the phone—collectors, creditors, and notices—made her feel smaller, more uncertain, and less prepared for the future.

As the days blurred together, her sadness deepened into something heavier: depression. She stopped answering calls, responding to texts, and reading emails. She ignored knocks at the door. It was easier to shut everything out than to admit how much she was struggling.

In her silence, she reminisced about old conversations with Jacob. They used to joke that they resided in a parallel universe—a realm composed of numbers, patterns, and improbable alignments that inexplicably led them back to each other. She recalled how he would sketch equations on napkins at diners, only to transform them into metaphors about love and risk. "You and me," he once said, tapping his pen against the paper, "we're the proof that variables can coexist without canceling each other out."

That was Jacob. To the world, he was pragmatic and reliable. To her, he was the mathematician of their romance. He demonstrated how order and affection could coexist, how logic and love weren't adversaries but partners in dance. Now, without him, the symmetry was shattered. Life felt like an unfinished equation that was unbalanced, incomplete, and unsolvable.

Just when she thought the imbalance might consume her entirely, a familiar knock sounded at the door. This one she couldn't ignore. It was Brad Silva.

Once a close colleague, Brad had witnessed her in command before—at StumbleTech, where she had transformed a struggling sales team into a success story, leading them from negative comp to over half a million dollars in sales in just seven months. He knew her talent firsthand. He respected her not only as a professional but as a leader with rare instincts. So yes, he had come to check on her, but he also had a plan.

Over a glass of wine at her kitchen table, Brad laid it out. "I need you to visit every store in my region," he said. "Provide me with your insights. My team is off track, and I need help. Your help."

Janis leaned back, giving him a slow once-over. "White shirt, striped tie, balanced knot... and the same dull shoes. You haven't changed a bit."

Brad chuckled, glancing down at his slacks. "Consistency is key."

"Or perhaps you simply detest shopping," she teased, her smile faint but genuine.

The brief exchange grounded her, as it served as proof that not everything in her world had shifted.

She gave a little shrug. "I understand, I'm not exactly in presentation mode."

Brad shook his head, dismissing the matter. "It doesn't matter. You still look like you...minus the colorful heels, of course."

Janis swirled the wine in her glass, observing the surface ripple. For weeks, her world had been a state of stagnation—heavy, suffocating, and devoid of motion. Brad's words stirred something within her that she hadn't experienced in months: a sense of movement.

Leaning back, her eyes weary yet clear, Janis addressed Brad. "Brad," she said, "I can't continue this. I'm stuck here alone, waiting for life to regain its meaning. A sinking ship doesn't need more water." Her voice trembled at the edges, but her resolve remained steadfast.

She acknowledged that grief would always hold a place in her story, but she also recognized that it couldn't be the sole chapter. Brad remained silent, allowing her to fill the void.

"I yearn for a way back into the world," Janis continued. "Not to escape what I've lost, but to demonstrate that I'm still here. That I can still stand, still fight, and still build something meaningful."

She glanced at him, searching his face for any sign of doubt. Instead, she found the unwavering confidence of a friend who believed in her more than she believed in herself.

However, one question lingered in her mind.

"When was the last time you spoke to Jackie?" she inquired.

She called me yesterday, but we didn't discuss much," Brad replied casually.

"So, she didn't pressure you into doing this?"

Brad shook his head. "Your sister is concerned, yes —but mostly, we just reminisced about college. Arguing over who had the correct answers on our Econ exams."

Janis offered a weary smile, her voice softening. She felt the weight within her shifting—not completely gone, but lighter, as if someone had reminded her that she was more than her grief. In that moment, she realized that it wasn't about ZinkaTech or even about saving Brad's team. It was about saving herself.

TURNING THE WHEEL

The introduction of Brad, the CEO of ZinkaTech, had been highly anticipated. The leadership team had been without a permanent head for quite some time, and the air carried a mix of curiosity, skepticism, and guarded hope. Some expected him to arrive alone, make a brief speech, and leave. Instead, he walked in with Janis.

He introduced her as his advisor, then paused, looked around the room, and made it clear that she would be leading the new change initiative. The announcement hit like a sudden gust—unexpected, heavy, and impossible to ignore.

Janis felt the full weight of Brad's expectations; she now wore the heaviest shoes in the room—shoes no one truly believed anyone could fill.

That skepticism made sense, because the leaders at QB-KOZE were already done with change. Not tired—done. Schedule changes, uniform changes, management rotations, process overhauls—they'd seen it all.

And every new initiative left them more cynical, more guarded, and less willing to try again. They weren't waiting for fresh ideas. They were waiting to see how long this new round would last before it collapsed like the others. Robin from the Petoskey location didn't wait to voice what everyone else was thinking.

She leaned back in her chair and made eye contact with Janis like she was daring her to respond. "Before you email me about changing this or that," she said, "Just know that I have a hundred unread emails in my 'Changes' folder—literally. I haven't even touched them. I've been here for twenty years. I'm pretty sure I know how to do my job."

Brad glanced at the board. The board looked at Brad. Brad looked at Janis, and Janis looked directly at Robin. The tension in the room went still. Let the drama begin, some thought. But Janis didn't flinch. She saw it not as a threat—but as an opportunity.

Years ago, a comment like Robin's might have unsettled her. But grief had taught her to slow time when it mattered. Instead of defending herself, she approached with a desire to learn, earn trust, and lead from the heart of the storm, not the sidelines.

"I appreciate your perspective, Robin," she replied calmly. "I believe there's truth to it. You're right—rapid change can be just as perilous as stagnation."

She paused, allowing the words to sink in. Then, she added, "Brad and I won't be demanding anyone to alter their identity or core values. However, we might ask you to modify your approach and methods. That's a different matter. It's not personal; it's the job."

Brad, who had worked with Janis before and understood her rhythm, interjected promptly. "The only way to turn around a large company is to seize control with both hands and execute swift action. Regardless of your role, everyone must recognize that the time for change isn't next year or next quarter. It's right now."

That's when Hanna from the Onaway location raised her hand. Her tone was not of defiance but rather exhaustion. "Brad," she said cautiously, "I understand this is your first day, but I'd like to share what truly frustrates us. It's not the hard work. It's that we spend weeks implementing changes based on a new idea, only to revert to our old practices two weeks later. There's no follow-through or commitment. It's all over the place. Our teams feel like trying something new is a waste of time."

Before Brad could respond, Janis spoke up. "There's nothing that frustrates me more," she said, "than selling something to my team only to turn around and sell them something else two weeks later."

She stood up and approached the group, her voice rising. "Turning the wheel," she continued, "doesn't mean spinning in circles. It means locking in direction, gripping with both hands, and making a strong, sustained turn. Everyone should feel it, even if it's uncomfortable."

Later that afternoon, Brad and Janis stepped outside for some fresh air. Brad leaned against her rental car. "Well," he said, "that could've gone much worse."

Janis smirked. "It could have. But it could also go exactly the same way next week if we don't change how we listen."

"You mean more heart, less pitch," he said.

"Exactly," she responded.

Back inside, the room remained tense. Some nodded, while a few stayed silent. One or two stared blankly, already deciding this was just another wave to wait out. Janis wasn't surprised. After all, steering a company off a cliff doesn't happen overnight, and neither does turning it around.

Janis adjusted the sleeves of her blazer and swept her gaze across the room as the second part of the meeting began. With her calm and composed demeanor, she captured the attention of the leaders gathered around the polished oak table.

"I've developed a plan to visit each of our stores," she announced, her voice steady but inviting. "These visits will be brief—no longer than a day at each location. My goal is to observe, understand, and assess without causing any disruptions."

A ripple of unease flickered through the room. Some leaders shifted in their seats, stealing quick glances at one another. The managers from underperforming stores seemed particularly restless, their expressions tightening with apprehension.

Undeterred, Janis continued. "To ensure transparency, I'll send calendar invites to each store manager ahead of time. This won't be a surprise visit. I believe in open communication and respect for your time and operations."

She paused briefly before adding, "And to be clear—I won't be showing up with a clipboard. I'm not there to catch mistakes. I'm coming to listen, to learn what's working, and to see the things your reports don't tell me."

That clarification slightly eased the tension in the room, but it didn't completely eliminate it.

She deliberately refrained from specifying what she was looking for, adding, "I prefer to observe the stores in their natural flow. Knowing specific criteria might unintentionally influence behaviors, and I want to experience each store's authentic environment."

The room fell silent, the weight of her words settling over the group. Some leaders nodded thoughtfully, while others wore thin masks of composure, their minds racing with potential consequences of her visits.

However, Janis wasn't oblivious. She didn't just hear the silence—she felt it. The subtle nervousness in the room wasn't about store visits. It was about something deeper: fatigue from scrutiny, fear of failure, and the fragile hope that maybe, just maybe, this time would be different.

She recognized that silence. Not as a red flag—but as a reflection. Janis observed the apprehension in the room, sensing the leaders' unease. It mirrored the vulnerability she once felt—the overwhelming weight of trying to stay afloat after her husband's passing. She recalled the late nights filled with unpaid bills, unanswered calls from creditors, and the suffocating feeling of falling behind with no clear path forward. That same heaviness was etched on the faces before her—not due to personal loss, but from the burden of unmet expectations, declining sales, and the fear of failure.

Drawing from that emotional reservoir, Janis took a quiet breath, grounding herself in authenticity. She stepped forward, her voice steady but filled with empathy.

"I recognize that look," she began softly, her gaze moving from one leader to the next. "It's the same look I had when I sat at my kitchen table, surrounded by bills I couldn't pay after my husband passed. The anxiety, the doubt, the sinking feeling that you're not enough—it's overwhelming. And it's not just about numbers or targets. It's about feeling like you're losing control."

A hush fell over the room as her words pierced through the corporate facade, striking a deep chord with those present.

Janis continued, "But here's what I learned—falling behind doesn't define you. It's what you do next that matters. I didn't overcome those struggles alone. I found strength in confronting the truth, leaning on others, and taking small, consistent steps forward. That's why I'm here—not to judge or criticize, but to stand with you, understand your struggles, and help us find a way through, together."

Her vulnerability created a ripple of connection. The tension eased, guarded expressions softened, and hesitant glances turned into engaged eye contact. By opening her heart, Janis didn't just ease their concerns —she inspired hope, making the leaders feel seen, understood, and ready to embrace the path ahead with renewed courage.

As the meeting closed, a subtle yet real shift took place. People didn't rush for the door. A few lingered to ask questions. Others stood a little taller. One or two even approached Janis privately to express their gratitude.

Later, as Janis packed up her things, she took one last look around the empty room. The wheel had turned—just a few degrees, and that's how momentum starts.

PART TWO

BATTLE FOR CHANGE

FLAGS OF NEGLECT

At dawn, Janis steered north toward Petoskey, the first store on her list. The freeway curved along the edge of the bay, and in the distance, the store's sign came into view—two letters burned out, the kind of quiet failure that dulls a brand's presence. As she drew closer, she noticed movement inside the hollow of one letter. Birds had nested there, twigs jutting outward like tiny flags of neglect. Clearly, this wasn't a one-day oversight, she thought.

She scanned the storefront for a moment. Her eyes tracing lines and clusters as if plotting a graph. A fast-food bag skittered across the pavement, carried by the breeze. Styrofoam cups leaned against the curb. Candy wrappers clung to the edge of the sidewalk. Near the trash can—already overflowing—lay the torn cardboard from a product package, the kind a customer might rip open on their way out.

Each item registered in her mind not as isolated debris, but as data points in a larger equation. Still out front, she could see the glass entrance door smudged with fingerprints. They caught the early light like a watermark on the store's standards. As she entered the store, the picture sharpened further: a hand truck resting against the wall, a small stack of empty boxes in the left corner. To the right, an aging signboard still advertised an event from months ago, its edges curled from the sun.

Only then did her mind begin to map it. Janis didn't just see trash, smudges, or burned-out lights. She saw variables gone wrong in a larger equation. A broken sign here, a neglected doorway there, a scatter of debris at the curb—together they formed a pattern, a distortion that rippled through the grid of the entire operation. To her, this wasn't cosmetic failure. It was the kind of imbalance that multiplies silently, until it reaches the customer.

Moving through the aisles, she cataloged each misaligned shelf. She did the same for each out-of-place display, cracked tile, and every product sitting dusty or abandoned. To Janis, the layout itself told a story: the flow of customers disrupted, attention diverted, opportunities for connection lost.

Even the team's behavior didn't escape her observation. She noticed how employees passed customers without acknowledgment, and how interactions—or the lack thereof—shifted the flow of engagement. Janis mentally plotted their energy and attentiveness against the environmental factors she'd already mapped. Subtle but telling patterns emerged: disengagement, frustration, a lack of cohesion.

Janis approached one of the customers herself. The employees watched quietly as she introduced herself and began a brief conversation.

"Hi, I'm Janis. Are you finding everything you need today?" she asked.

The customer looked toward a small display. "I saw this ad for a thumb drive, and I need one—but I also need a router. I'm not sure which one to get."

"Let's take a look," Janis said, walking with the customer to the router section.

She pointed out a couple of options, explaining which would best fit their needs, then retrieved a compatible thumb drive from the shelf. By the time she returned to the main aisle, her notebook was a web of observations.

Robin stepped out of the office and asked gently, "Can I assist you during your walk?"

Janis smiled and shook her head. "Thank you, but I'd prefer to walk the store alone first. I like to predict which departments are performing well or struggling based on what I see—merchandising, stock levels, how the displays are positioned. It's a method I enjoy before looking at actual sales numbers."

Robin nodded, curiosity flickering across her face. Then, lowering her voice, she added, "When you're ready, I'd like to introduce you to the team. They've heard someone new would be coming in, and it will help them to know why you're here."

"I'd like that," Janis replied.

Robin gestured toward a group of associates working the floor. A few cast cautious glances in Janis's direction.

"Everyone," Robin said, raising her voice just enough, "this is Janis Harbinger. She's here to help us take a close look at how we're running the store. Please make her feel welcome as she walks through."

The team offered polite nods and smiles, though uncertainty lingered in their expressions. Janis returned the gesture warmly, choosing not to linger but to keep observing quietly. She wasn't here to lecture. Not yet.

A voice from the back called for Robin. She excused herself abruptly. Her stride brisk as she disappeared toward the office corridor. The tension in her movements seemed off, Janis thought. Perhaps someone important hadn't been told about the visit. That realization set another variable in motion. In Robin's absence, the words began to flow.

"If there was a contest for who could turn a good day into a bad day the fastest, Robin would win, every time," one associate muttered.

"She's so process-focused that it's like she has tunnel vision. No emotional intelligence. Doesn't listen, doesn't communicate. Just reacts," another said.

"She's bitter too, about her lack of growth, and that bitterness... it trickles down. It makes the place feel unsafe sometimes," a third added.

"And Carl, he's... well, he's emotionless. Like he's checked out," one team member admitted. "There's this detachment about him that makes it hard to connect or rely on him."

"He lacks leadership skills," another added. "He doesn't pay attention to the details that keep the store running smoothly. Sometimes it feels like he doesn't even understand the processes we're supposed to follow."

A few exchanged glances before someone else chimed in, "He's clueless about laws, safety rules— things that could get us in serious trouble. And he's way too laid back. No one ever gets held accountable around here."

"Always on vacation," muttered a voice from the back. "Nice guy, sure, but there's a cynicism that comes with that too."

Janis observed silently, taking in the layers of concern and the subtle ways their words painted a picture of leadership gaps that went beyond surface issues. This wasn't just about personalities, it was about a store desperately needing direction and care.

Carl wandered over to see who had captured the team's attention. It was obvious he hadn't checked the calendar, as he seemed genuinely unaware that a visitor was coming. His uniform was wrinkled and a bit disheveled; another small clue in a growing pattern that the standard for presentation was either undefined or unenforced.

Janis greeted him with warmth and professionalism, masking any reaction to the candid criticisms she had just heard. She introduced herself, explained her role, and described her mission to help the store improve.

Carl smirked and made an off-color joke about the company sending "the new girl" to spy on them. Janis let the remark roll past her, responding with a polite laugh before guiding the conversation back toward her assessment. Internally, she noted the defensiveness under the humor—a signal worth remembering.

Janis carefully noted the positives, and there were many worth recognizing. Loyal customers, well-maintained displays, and a handful of departments that reflected genuine effort and pride. But the negatives, though fewer, cast a far larger shadow. Merchandise felt uninviting, dust coating even the high-ticket items. The bathrooms told an even harsher story: a filthy toilet, grimy floors, an empty towel dispenser.

In the backroom, boxes sat unscanned and piled carelessly, evidence that processes had unraveled long ago. Each of these issues wasn't just a slip—it was a fracture in the foundation.

After reviewing the break room and stepping outside to inspect the back parking lot, she made her way to Robin's office. There, she thanked Robin for hosting her and encouraged her to reach out with any questions.

Janis deliberately chose not to share her observations just yet. It wasn't about withholding—it was about protecting the clarity of her process. She needed space to weigh what she had seen against the store's metrics and to separate her initial impressions from the emotions in the room. Grace, she knew, wasn't just about kindness. It was about restraint.

On her way to the car, Janis noticed the trash was still sitting out front, unchanged since her arrival. The same debris still littered the parking lot, as if the day had passed without anyone seeing it—or caring to.

Driving toward her next location, she felt a quiet ache for the team she was leaving behind. It wasn't frustration; it was compassion. Despite everything she had seen and heard, she still carried hope for each person in that store. She didn't believe in giving up on people. She knew she could work with anyone. Win with anyone.

Her mind replayed the faces she'd encountered that day. With each one, she began sketching ideas—small, specific ways she could help them grow, regain their footing, and rediscover what was possible. For Janis, improvement wasn't just about fixing a store. It was about restoring people.

POLISHED STRAIN

The drive to the Onaway store felt like a shift in atmosphere before she even stepped out of the car. The parking lot was spotless, free of the trash and clutter she'd seen earlier that day. The glass entrance gleamed as though it had been cleaned that morning. From the outside, this store was entirely on brand, as it appeared sharp, welcoming, and professional.

Inside, the impression continued. Bright, well-lit aisles shaped the flow of the store, and the air carried the hum of quiet productivity. Customers were being greeted at the door, and Janis herself received a warm welcome. This team knew she was coming. The manager, Hanna, had been waiting near the cash register all day, ready for her arrival. The staff, all in uniform, looked neat, polished, and prepared.

Janis explained the purpose of her visit and began her assessment. At first glance, the store seemed nearly flawless—until she noticed customers wandering the aisles alone.

Then she spotted a deeper problem: missing price tags on key products. Without clear pricing, questions were inevitable. Yet the staff were so absorbed in project work that few had time to assist. Not even Janis's questions were answered. Clearly, customers were being quietly underserved.

When Janis asked Hanna about her staffing, the truth surfaced quickly. Turnover was high. Salaries were low. Few applicants wanted to work every weekend. When Janis complimented the store's cleanliness, Hanna admitted she handled most of it herself, often working open to close, six days a week.

That relentless schedule left her little time for training, and Hanna knew her own shortcomings. She described herself as unmotivated, undertrained, lacking leadership skills, and sometimes a poor communicator. She admitted her attitude could slip on hard days. She also confessed to feeling nervous, even scared at times. However, she was great with customers, deeply sympathetic, and fiercely competitive. It struck Janis how much Hanna resembled the store itself—flawless on the outside, carrying hidden strain within.

"I'll do the best I can to get you some help," Janis told her, meaning every word.

As Janis continued her assessment, the picture came into sharper focus. She was surrounded by doers

—people who kept the wheels turning, shelves stocked, and tasks checked off—but not by salespeople. Transactions were happening, yes, but only because customers were making them happen.

Those who already knew exactly what they wanted found it, paid for it, and left. Those willing to gamble on their own guesswork took the risk and bought anyway. But anyone in that uncertain middle ground —unsure of what to choose or why—drifted out the door empty-handed. It tied directly back to what she'd seen earlier. Employees were too busy with projects to answer her questions, much less a customer's. She underlined the point in her notes. This wasn't just a staffing problem, it was a sales culture gap.

She moved toward the front of the store, her pen still in hand, and caught a moment at checkout that made her pause. A cashier had just wrapped up what seemed like a warm, personal conversation with a customer. The kind that could make someone feel recognized and valued. But then, just like that, it was over—no "thank you for shopping with us," no "we hope to see you again," no celebration of the sale at all. A moment of connection had slipped away without leaving a lasting mark.

Then Hanna stepped in. Not to intervene unnecessarily, but with a quiet, practiced intuition. She greeted the next customer with attentiveness, asked thoughtful questions, and noticed the little cues others missed. One shopper hesitated in the toy aisle—Hanna asked about their needs, pointed out a hidden promotion, and guided them toward a confident choice. The sale was small, but the interaction left a visible ripple: the customer relaxed, smiled, and moved on satisfied. Janis made a note in the margin.

Hanna sees what others overlook.
She can read the room, adjust on the fly,
and make people feel seen.

It wasn't just competence, but instead, subtle and undeniable leadership potential. A few minutes later, Janis overheard two team members venting to a customer. The customer, in turn, felt compelled to share her own negative work stories. The danger in this didn't escape Janis—when customers start sharing your pain, they might also start avoiding it.

As she watched these conversations unfold, she saw more than a sales gap—she saw people trying to survive under pressure. She knew that feeling too well. When she had been drowning in her own pain and personal struggles, Brad had shown up for her. He hadn't judged her, or written her off. He had quietly and intentionally stepped in to help her find her footing again. That memory still carried weight.

Now, standing in Brad's shoes, Janis felt that same pull. This wasn't just about fixing a store. It was about repaying a debt of grace. Hanna needed someone to stand in the gap for her the way Brad had once done for Janis. That thought kept her moving, as she diligently took notes, not to criticize but to prepare a path forward. Before she left, Janis made the following observations:

- Aisle congestion near seasonal items – (Janis thought: "It's hard to sell what people can't comfortably shop. Layout is stealing sales here.")
- No visible upsell prompts at the register – (Janis thought: "This is free money left on the counter. All it takes is one question: 'Would you like…?'")
- Damaged packaging left on shelves – (Janis thought: "If I see this, customers definitely see it —and they'll wonder what else is neglected.")
- Backroom door left propped open – (Janis thought: "Not only unsafe, but unattractive.")
- Aisle signs inconsistent or outdated – (Janis thought: "Signage should not be confusing.")

On the way to the door, Janis turned back to Hanna. "Thank you for your time today," she said. "I know things are tough right now, but I want you to know— you've got good people here. People worth investing in. Brad and I are planning a two-day off-site meeting with all the store managers in about two months. It's not a tear-you-down meeting—it's about growth, encouragement, and building each other up. We want to take what we've learned from the field and figure out, together, the direction we need to go. We'll get there as a team."

Hanna gave a tired but genuine smile. It wasn't a solution yet, but it was the beginning of one. Janis was aware that with the right opportunity and guidance, Hanna had the potential to grow in ways she hadn't even imagined. Brad would also recognize this when the time came.

As Janis stepped outside into the clean and quiet parking lot, she couldn't help but feel a sense of anticipation. That meeting would be more than an exchange of numbers and strategies. For some, it might be the moment everything shifted.

A SOFT FLAME

As Janis closed the door on the seventh and final store, a heavy quiet settled over her. She carried with her the faces, the voices, and all the moments of frustration that lingered longer than she expected. These weren't just stores struggling to meet goals; these were teams, people, each wrestling with invisible burdens.

Everywhere Janis turned, the pattern repeated itself. Teams were fractured, stretched too thin, and unsure if anyone was truly listening. Each day, employees showed up, dedicated yet drained, trying to contain chaos without the tools or the support they needed. What was missing wasn't just talent; it was trust, belief, and the spirit that keeps people moving forward. Janis knew that when spirit falters, everything else follows.

The merchandise spoke its own language. Forgotten promises lingered on shelves where products sat untouched. At the same time, the very items customers wanted most were absent or hidden from sight. Layouts meant to welcome instead confused, transforming simple paths into mazes that dulled curiosity instead of sparking it. Janis could feel the resistance customers must have felt: subtle, invisible barriers that pushed them away.

Short-term fixes had built up like quicksand. Half-finished price tags, outdated signage, and sales that sounded more like noise than opportunity piled on top of each other. A missing price tag was not trivial; it chipped away at trust and left customers uncertain. Poor lighting threw cold shadows into corners, making them look deserted and unsafe. Behind it all, broken logistics created frustration with late trucks, misplaced stock, and frantic restocking at the last possible moment.

Then there were the people. Faces were etched with exhaustion, yet many still carried a spark of pride. They were caught in an unforgiving cycle: opening late while customers waited outside, leaving carts stranded in the lot, and neglecting displays that should have been tended. Janis felt the pull of their unspoken plea for rest and recognition.

"Janis, you perceive what others fail to see," Brad had once told her. The truth of his words pressed down on her now. What she carried was not simply an eye for detail; it was the ability to see the heart beneath the struggle and the possibility hidden in the mess. That was why Brad had chosen her. Not to list problems but to imagine paths forward.

Even with that trust behind her, doubt knotted in her chest. These were not minor cracks; the foundation itself was shaking. Could she, with all she knew, really help these teams steady themselves? Was there enough time? Was there enough hope?

She closed her notebook slowly, letting herself breathe in that uncertainty. The answers wouldn't be found in charts or numbers alone. They'd come from people—the leaders scared to ask for help, the teams desperate to believe change was possible, the quiet strength waiting to be rediscovered.

Yet beneath the weight pressing down, a soft flame of resolve sparked within her. Ahead lay the next step: a two-day off-site meeting with all the store managers. This wouldn't be a place for blame or judgment. It would be a space for healing, encouragement, and honest talk. A chance to turn the lessons of the field into a shared vision for the future.

That meeting, carefully planned with Brad, carried the promise of a turning point. Hope could take root again, and scattered pieces might finally come together. Janis looked ahead, fully aware of the challenges, yet she also recognized something stronger than the obstacles: the possibility of shared strength. If leaders chose to rise and teams dared to believe, the foundation could ultimately be rebuilt.

SILENT WITNESSES

Janis understood that walking the floors of these stores was only the first step. The true story lay hidden in the data, tucked inside spreadsheets, surveys, resumes, and reports. She sought solitude in a quiet room, surrounded by these silent witnesses to the stores' realities. Each file, each number, offered a thread she could follow to uncover deeper truths.

She began with the metrics, clear reflections of how the stores were performing. Sales figures highlighted both successes and failures. Foot traffic showed interest, but it often did not translate into purchases. Conversion rates varied by location, yet one pattern was consistent: visitors left without finding what they needed. These numbers were more than statistics; they represented real people's unmet needs.

Next, she reviewed customer service surveys. Shoppers' voices were candid, blending praise with criticism. Warm greetings were sometimes overshadowed by busy employees. Aisles were cluttered and confusing. Questions went unanswered, and needs were ignored. These comments confirmed what Janis had observed on the floors. Collectively, they offered a roadmap for rebuilding trust and improving the experience.

To dig deeper, she reviewed resumes and hiring records. Hires often did not match the demands of the roles. People were placed out of necessity rather than fit. Gaps in hiring and support made it hard to attract and retain talent. The flawed system created wounds that kept reopening.

Janis then turned to employee engagement surveys to understand the staff. The results painted a sobering picture. Many employees felt overworked, undervalued, and unseen. Managers were often distant or ineffective. Morale was low, and turnover was high. Staff worked hard despite minimal guidance and support. They were people with hopes, fears, and talents that had yet to be nurtured.

Janis then examined the merchandising plans. On paper, they were carefully drafted, but in practice, many were outdated. Some store layouts no longer matched the plans, yet merchandise continued to arrive without adequate shelf space. Products would be sent one month and discontinued the next, confusing customers and frustrating employees.

Deliveries were often mistimed, with some arriving too early and others too late, making organization in the backroom nearly impossible. Teams struggled to keep up, and scheduling enough staff was a constant challenge. Many employees worked short shifts and needed second jobs to make a living, yet overtime was often required to manage the store's demands. This made it difficult for managers to ensure coverage and keep operations running smoothly.

Her attention shifted beyond the store walls to the communities each location served. Every neighborhood was a unique ecosystem with its own culture, economy, and expectations. A one-size-fits-all approach ignored these differences. Opportunities to connect were missed. Product selection, store atmosphere, and marketing often failed to reflect the local community. This disconnect extended from the customer to employees and back again.

The picture was complex but coherent. The stores' challenges were not isolated faults; they were symptoms of a fractured system. Fixing it required more than checklists. It demanded empathy, strategic thinking, and a deep understanding of human nature.

Janis leaned back and let the information settle. Leading change meant more than technical fixes. It required courage to face discomfort, patience to build trust, and humility to listen before speaking. These were the true tools of transformation, and she was ready to wield them.

Even with that readiness, a whisper of doubt lingered. Could these changes reach every store and every employee before the window of opportunity closed? The weight pressed down, but it also fueled determination.

The path ahead remained uncertain. For every lost sale and weary employee, there was a chance to build something better. Janis would find the way, one step at a time.

PART THREE

PATTERNS IN THE DARK

THE BURIED PAST

To the surprise of Brad—and even more so to Karen Huntley, the head of HR—Janis requested the résumés of the company's upper management. At first, the request drew little pushback. It seemed practical, even harmless, given the scope of her assessment. Most executives had impressive histories, notable credentials, and decades of leadership experience. On paper, they were the kind of team any company would be proud to showcase.

That perception shifted the moment word of her request reached the executives. Quiet concern rippled through the ranks, whispered behind closed doors. Soon, HR contacted Brad directly, polite in tone yet tinged with unease.

Brad later appeared at Janis's office, pausing in the doorway just long enough to signal that this was no casual visit.

"Got a minute?" he asked.

His voice sounded friendly, but Janis recognized the underlying invitation: explain yourself.

She smiled, keeping her tone calm. "I just want to get a clearer picture of the leadership team—their backgrounds, experience, and career paths."

Brad studied her for a long moment, skepticism etched in his expression. He didn't speak immediately, letting the silence stretch.

Finally, he gave a slight nod. "Alright. Just... keep me informed," he said, his caution still lingering.

Janis waited until he left, letting the pause settle her thoughts. Then, with the résumés finally in hand, she began tracing each career backward, digging into the companies where these leaders had once held power. At first, nothing seemed out of the ordinary. Then, subtle shadows began to seep through, hinting at hidden stories and secrets buried in the past.

David Milford, the Area Manager for QB-KOZE, had resigned from his previous position as CEO due to a scandal involving an affair with a minor. The story had been suppressed to safeguard his former company's image, but the internet never forgets.

Chuck McClung's name surfaced next. He had been forced out of an earlier leadership position amid allegations of misappropriating company funds. Janis reflected on the company's recent history—the data breach that had shaken customers long before her arrival. Perhaps Chuck was the leader alluded to in some of the negative reviews she had read, or perhaps it was another executive entirely. Either way, the pattern of risky leadership was clear, and she understood how easily it could repeat itself.

The most unexpected discovery came from an old photograph buried deep within a local business association's online archive. Karen Huntley smiled beside Milford and McClung at what appeared to be a charity gala. This was years before any of them had joined the company.

David's hand rested lightly at Karen's waist. Chuck's grip on her shoulder was firm. All three appeared flushed—perhaps even intoxicated. Stranger yet, each wore apparel branded with the same company logo. Something seems off, Janis thought. And yet, in the present, they passed one another in the hallway with barely a nod, as if no history existed between them. That contrast was what unsettled her most. If she mishandled the discovery, it could raise questions about her judgment. But if she ignored it, she risked allowing cultural rot to spread. Her reputation—and perhaps her chance at becoming CEO —rested on what she chose to do next.

She decided not to mention the photo to Karen or Brad, instead saving it quietly as another piece of the larger puzzle. Still, the image lingered in her mind, carrying a weight she couldn't easily set aside.

One pattern, though, was already unmistakable: the company hadn't just lost market share; it had lost grace. And without grace, survival was nearly impossible. Customers today, she reminded herself, have countless options: online retailers, and marketplaces just a click away. Love for the brand is the only reason anyone chooses one over the other. That love cannot be bought, she thought. It must be earned. Janis opened her notebook and began jotting down ways to earn it back, letting her mind move quickly across the page.

Fighting poverty and hunger.
Protecting clean water.
Combating climate change.
Supporting education.
Advancing healthcare.
Defending human rights.
Standing with communities in crisis.

Each phrase was both a reminder and a commitment—anchors for rebuilding trust. Only by rooting their brand in real, meaningful action could they regain the trust that had slipped away. Only then would customers see them not just as a store, but as a force for good—worthy of loyalty, respect, and a place in their lives again.

Janis knew this was the only path forward. After all, without grace, no brand can survive—and with it, almost anything is possible.

THE SUMMONS

J anis typed out the email invitation for the mandatory offsite meeting.

Subject: Mandatory Offsite Meeting – Leadership and Performance Alignment

Body:
We will be meeting offsite on Thursday, June 27th at 9:00 a.m. to address the state of our performance and the path forward.

This session is mandatory for all managers and key leaders. Together, we'll focus on building stronger alignment, improving our results, and preparing for the opportunities ahead. She clicked send to finalize the message before anxiety could claim her thoughts. For a moment she lingered, aware of the replies that might flood her inbox. Each could carry questions or complaints, but she was prepared to face them. She closed her laptop and headed down the hall to the break room.

She grabbed her store-bought salad from the fridge and bought a bottle of green tea from the vending machine. Her gum she pinched in a napkin, then arced it toward the trash. As usual, her jump shot was good on Friday. With that small win, she strolled down the hallway again.

With lunch in hand, she pushed open the door to the small conference room on the west side of the building. She set her food down and unzipped her office bag, readying herself for the conversation ahead.

Brad was already there at the table, pen in hand, his thumb clicking it again and again. The sound was sharp in the quiet room, a nervous tic she'd noticed before. She wondered if he realized how much it gave him away. She slipped into the chair across from him, the silence stretching long enough to make the first words matter.

"I'm curious," he said, looking up. "What's your vision for this project?"

Janis reached into her bag and pulled out her notes. Each store had its own folder, filled with weeks of research and careful analysis. She arranged them neatly on the table, keeping the red folder apart from the rest.

"Brad, I believe some of our leaders have grown detached. They no longer see their stores or their teams as they truly are," she said. "We must awaken them—but not through humiliation. It has to be presented with truth and a clear path forward."

He leaned back in his chair. "So, you intend to strike a delicate balance—presenting harsh realities while keeping them willing to engage?"

"Yes. Data and inspiration. The metrics tell us what's happening; the stories reveal why it's happening. If I present only one, half the room disengages."

Brad scribbled a note. "So, this is both a cultural reset and a system reset."

"Exactly. Attention to detail will be enforced through coaching. Managers will be moved based on talent, not tenure. Promotions will be earned through skill, not familiarity. And before we train, we must identify what actually needs to be taught."

Janis paused, her hand brushing the red folder she had kept apart. She slid it across the table.

Brad opened it and studied the black-and-white photo inside. "Where did you get this?"

"I found it online. I stumbled across it while tracking the bigwigs last week. Something about it caught my eye."

His eyes narrowed slightly, though his voice remained even. "Interesting."

He set the photo down gently, as if it carried more weight than it appeared. "Let's focus on the meeting for now. I'll revisit this later."

Janis exhaled, lowering her voice. "Brad... I know I can lead this, but I worry about the board's reaction. If I make even a minor mistake, they'll see it as weakness. I can't afford that. My goal is to lead one of these acquisitions—maybe even step into a CEO role someday."

Brad looked at her steadily. "Janis, you have the vision, the instincts, and the discipline. I've watched you analyze, teach, and execute in ways most people can't even imagine. The team will follow you because they trust you. You're more than capable."

She gave a small, tense smile. "Still, it feels like one misstep could derail everything."

"Then treat this like a rehearsal, not a performance," Brad said, nodding. "Show them their potential. You don't have to carry the weight of the world alone. That's leadership—lifting others without losing yourself."

They spent the next hour mapping the flow: when to present key data, when to pause for discussion, when to challenge without demoralizing. By the time they stood, the plan was sharp, but the stakes felt heavier.

As Janis gathered her things, she whispered, "If you can lead them with true grace, they'll follow you through whatever comes."

Brad gave a firm nod. "And if anyone can, it's you."

ECHOES OF JACOB

Janis sat in the small exam room, hands resting on her lap, fingers twisting the edge of a tissue she hadn't yet needed. The room was quiet—too quiet—but her thoughts were loud, colliding with each other, refusing to line up. She had been called in that morning. Her doctor's voice on the phone had carried a weight she recognized but had never wanted aimed at her.

The door opened. Dr. Gannenburg stepped in slowly, folder in hand, her eyes softened by what they carried.

"Janis," she said gently, closing the door, "thank you for coming in so quickly."

Janis nodded, throat dry. "Your voice on the phone... I knew it wasn't just a routine follow-up."

Dr. Gannenburg set the folder down and pulled her stool closer. "I wish I could tell you it was nothing. But the biopsy results confirm stage two breast cancer."

She paused, giving the words space. "It's localized—we caught it before it spread beyond the lymph nodes—but we'll need to move quickly."

The word cancer rang in Janis's ears like an alarm that wouldn't shut off. She drew in a breath, then another, gripping the tissue tighter.

"I remember when you sat across from me years ago," Dr. Gannenburg said, her tone softer still. "But that time it wasn't your diagnosis—it was Jacob's."

Janis's eyes softened at his name. "He was so strong," she whispered. "Even in the middle of it, he kept thinking about his patients."

"He was remarkable," Dr. Gannenburg agreed, reverence in her voice. "We worked in the same building for over a decade. I saw firsthand how he carried himself—fit, sharp, humble. I remember how you two would stop by my office after a shift, him with that easy smile, asking about my day before talking about his own."

Tears welled in Janis's eyes. "He used to say every patient deserved the best we had—whether it was medical expertise or just a kind word."

Dr. Gannenburg reached out, covering Janis's hand with hers. "And I think he would want you to give yourself that same kindness now."

She opened the folder. "For treatment, we have options. At this stage, we can consider breast-conserving surgery—a lumpectomy—followed by radiation. Or a mastectomy if you prefer a more aggressive approach. Chemotherapy may be part of the plan depending on further testing. There are hormone therapies if your cancer is estrogen-receptor positive, and we'll also check HER2 status, which could open up targeted treatments."

Janis nodded, trying to follow the words, but they dissolved into the louder thought: This is really happening.

"I know the road ahead isn't what you planned," Dr. Gannenburg said, leaning closer. "Especially with your work, with everything else on your plate. But I've seen you walk through harder things. You stood by Jacob through every round, every test, every hard night. You know the terrain—and now you must walk it for yourself."

Tears spilled, not from fear alone, but from the sudden memory of Jacob's steady hand in hers in rooms just like this. "I just wish he were here to tell me it's going to be okay."

"I think," Dr. Gannenburg said softly, "he already has—just in the way he lived, and in the way you carry him with you."

The ride home was a blur. She barely remembered pulling out of the clinic parking lot—only that her hands gripped ten and two, and the road stretched longer than it had that morning. Words from the office looped in her mind—stage two... localized... move quickly—until they were no longer sentences but a low pressure against her chest.

The late afternoon sun threw long slants of light across the highway. She kept her sunglasses on, though no one was there to see her eyes. It gave her the illusion of control, as if she could hide from the truth by keeping her gaze fixed and her jaw tight.

When she reached her driveway, she sat for a moment in the stillness of the car, keys cooling in her hand. She told herself to move, to step inside, to carry on with the day. Instead, she closed her eyes and let the tears come—not deep sobs, but quiet, measured ones that left no trace.

That night, the house was dark and silent, but sleep would not come. She lay on her back staring at the ceiling, the faint tick of the clock marking each stubborn minute. Her mind spun through images— Jacob in the hospital, the moment of his diagnosis, the smile he had forced through the pain, telling her it would be okay even when they both knew it wouldn't.

She could tell Brad. He'd know what to say—or at least know how to listen. But the thought of adding that weight to his shoulders, just weeks before the offsite, made her press her lips together. No. She would carry this alone, at least until the meeting was behind them.

Still, in the quiet, she wondered how long she could keep the two worlds separate: the capable leader guiding a team through change, and the woman counting days and appointments, waiting for results.

OPEN EYES

In the days after Janis announced the offsite meeting, the work was suffocating. Everything blurred together—she needed to breathe, but barely could. Brad noticed the subtle changes first: the tired lines under her eyes, the rare slip in her usual sharpness, the quiet sighs she tried to hide.

One afternoon, he found her alone in the conference room, pouring over a thick stack of notes with little focus.

"Janis," he said softly, stepping closer. "I want to help. How about I take the lead on the section about Leading Through Change? It could ease your load."

Her expression brightened with surprise before a grateful smile broke through her exhaustion. "That would mean more than you know."

Brad rubbed his beard. "And the customer service section—I think Hanna should take that."

Janis blinked, hesitation flashing across her face. "Hanna? But that's where she and her team have been struggling."

"That's exactly why," Brad said firmly. "It's a real growth opportunity for her. Hanna has hidden strength we haven't fully tapped yet. I'll back her every step of the way. I'll call her and explain what we need."

He picked up his phone and called Hanna. Janis watched as he spoke quietly, listening intently.

"Hanna," Brad said once the line connected, "we want you to lead the customer service section for the offsite presentation. I know it's a big responsibility, but it's also a chance to showcase your skills. You won't be alone—you'll have support and guidance throughout the process."

A pause followed, then Hanna's voice came, tinged with hesitation. "Customer service? That's... the area where my team and I are struggling the most. Are you sure?"

Brad's tone remained steady. "Exactly why this is the right challenge. We've seen what you're capable of —you just need the opportunity. I'll guide you through questions, and Janis will coordinate the broader strategy."

Hanna drew in a breath, weighing the weight of the responsibility. "Alright... I'll do it," she said finally, her voice steadier than she felt.

When the call ended, Janis exhaled, a mix of relief and concern swirling inside her. She knew the work would be intense, but she could see the spark this challenge might ignite. It's moments like these that open our eyes, she thought, realizing how much potential was waiting to be uncovered.

True to her nature, Hanna threw herself into the work with fierce determination. In her store, she combed through customer surveys, analyzed feedback, and studied best practices from successful teams outside the company. She reached out to frontline employees, listening carefully, absorbing their frustrations and ideas.

Gradually, the fog began to lift. Hanna uncovered patterns beneath the noise and started seeing solutions. In team meetings at the store, she found her voice—speaking up with confidence, proposing concrete steps based on real research and honest conversations. Her team noticed the change.

Hanna was no longer just a manager struggling to keep pace. She had become a key player, injecting fresh energy and practical insight into a team desperate for change. As the offsite drew closer, she joined virtual calls with Janis and Brad, reviewing progress, refining strategies, and discussing next steps. Janis allowed herself a quiet smile, recognizing the transformation. This is why we invest in people, she thought. This is why we push, even when it's hard.

CROSSCURRENTS

About a week before the meeting, Brad walked down to Karen's office. He paused in the doorway, his tone even but direct.

"Do you have a moment?"

Karen looked up from her desk and nodded. Brad stepped inside, closed the door behind him, and laid a photo on the desk between them.

"This came up," he said quietly.

Karen's eyes fell to the image. Her composure slipped. Brad studied her reaction. His first thought went back to the company's data breach—the blow that had damaged ZinkaTech's reputation before he ever arrived. The photo wasn't as severe, but it carried the same shadow of risk: a reminder of how quickly small things could spiral. Karen shifted in her chair, shame crossing her features. Brad noticed. He didn't press. Instead, he softened his tone.

"I understand, Karen. I know you didn't intend for this." He let the words settle, then added, "Let's just be careful."

He slowly straightened his tie. "We'll leave it there."

Without another word, he stepped out—gracefully, without piling on—leaving Karen alone with the weight of her thoughts.

The office felt heavier once he was gone. Karen sat in silence, staring at the blinds as the late afternoon sun cut across her desk. Guilt pressed against her chest —not because of Brad's words, but because she knew he was right. Some wounds from the past still lingered, and the last thing the company needed was another reminder.

She drew in a slow breath and reached for her phone. If there was going to be a way forward, she couldn't carry the burden alone.

"David," she said when he picked up, her voice steady but edged with urgency. "Can you and Chuck meet me at Café Merlot? It's important."

When they arrived, Karen was already waiting at a small table tucked into the corner. The café's low hum of conversation gave them just enough cover. She motioned for them to sit, hands folded neatly on the table, her face composed but serious.

David slid into the seat across from her, Chuck beside him. Both leaned in, sensing the weight in her expression.

Karen lowered her voice. "I need to talk with you— off the record."

David and Chuck exchanged a glance.

"There's a photo circulating," Karen said. "One of my friends posted it on social media and tagged me. I didn't think much of it at the time, but it's become a problem."

David frowned. "What kind of photo?"

Karen hesitated. "It's an older picture—one with me and both of you. I'm pretty sure Janis found it while digging online. She's the only one who would even bring it up."

Chuck's brow furrowed. "Wait, how long has this been around? Why didn't we know?"

Karen's eyes dropped before she answered. "Because I thought it would stay buried. Honestly, I tried to keep our relationships quiet during the hiring process. I pretended I didn't know you both, to avoid accusations of favoritism. But that's not the only issue."

She drew in a breath, voice tightening. "My husband doesn't know I was at that party. That night, I told him I was at my mother's. If this photo makes the rounds, it could create problems at home too. He already has questions about loyalty. This would only deepen them."

The words lingered, heavier than she intended. David sat back slightly, jaw tightening. For a moment, he thought of his own wife—the sharp questions she asked whenever his schedule didn't match the calendar, the way her eyes lingered just a little too long on his phone when it buzzed. Trust, once strong, now fragile.

Beside him, Chuck's gaze dropped to the table. He wasn't proud of how many dinners he'd missed lately, how often his wife's smile seemed more polite than warm. Hearing Karen admit her fear struck something uncomfortably close.

David cleared his throat, breaking the silence. "That could make things worse if it comes out."

Karen nodded. "Exactly. If this comes up at the meeting—or anywhere else—we have to be upfront and tell the truth. No hiding. I can't afford to spin this, not here, not at home."

Chuck rubbed his chin thoughtfully. "So we own it. No spin, no dodging. You know I like to stay off the radar. I'm not like this guy,"—he gestured toward David with a small smirk—"always poking and prodding."

David shot back with a grin. "Yeah, like when you fell asleep in the meeting and I had to wake you up."

Chuck leaned back slightly, shrugging. "I'm a company guy. I love what Janis is doing, which is why I stop by her desk every day and ask if she needs help. Keeps me in the loop."

David shook his head, lips tight. "Well, some of the stuff the company comes up with is a bunch of crap, and I just can't support it. I won't pretend it's all brilliant."

Chuck met his gaze. "I get that. But I'm in this for the long haul. Janis is making moves that actually matter. If I can help, I will. No matter what."

David raised his brow. "Okay. We face it together."

Karen exhaled, tension easing just a bit. "Good. I wanted you to hear it from me first."

The conversation left David and Chuck uneasy—not only about the meeting, but about the silent reminders of their own fragile ground at home.

Back at the office in the days that followed, that tension surfaced. Karen's demeanor toward Janis shifted—polite but distant, professional but cold. She caught herself hesitating before approaching Janis in the hallway. The woman who had once been welcoming—even inviting Janis to lunch during those first days at the company—now seemed like a stranger.

Karen told herself she had every right to feel unsettled. After all, Janis had dug into her past, uncovered that photo, and shown it to Brad. To Karen, it felt petty—a breach of unspoken trust.

When Karen finally spoke, her tone was careful, professional but clipped. "Janis, I wanted to see how you're holding up with everything going on."

Janis looked up, steady and composed, sensing something unspoken behind the words. "Thank you, Karen. I'm doing my best. It's a lot to manage, but I'm focused."

Karen nodded, offering a tight smile that didn't quite reach her eyes. "Good. That's important."

Janis studied Karen's expression, searching for the warmth that had once been there. Instead, she found a reserved politeness, as if a wall had quietly risen between them. She wondered what she had done to deserve it. Was it the photo? Had Karen learned about her diagnosis and was pulling away for her own reasons?

But Janis refused to let suspicion breed bitterness. She kept her voice calm and gracious. "If there's anything I can do to help, or if you want to talk, I'm here."

Karen hesitated, then shook her head. "No, I think we're good. Just... busy times."

Behind the carefully measured words, Karen wrestled with frustration. She wanted to confront Janis, to tell her how the photo felt like a betrayal, but professionalism held her tongue. Instead, she chose distance—enough to protect herself, but not enough to burn bridges.

Janis left their brief exchange with a knot in her stomach, but also a quiet resolve. I won't let this distraction break me. I have bigger things to face.

Brad noticed the shift. He watched quietly, never pressing but always ready. He made sure Janis had coffee in the morning, volunteered to run reports, and took on parts of the presentation to lighten her load. His steady, silent support became her anchor amid the uncertainty.

The contrast between Brad's warmth and Karen's coolness was stark. Janis felt caught between two worlds—one of encouragement, the other of cautious distance.

Through it all, Hanna's progress shone like a beacon—a hopeful sign that change was possible. But the rest of the office carried a different mood. Brad, Janis, and even Hanna found themselves on the receiving end of a quiet chill. The upcoming meeting had cast a shadow of uncertainty. People were still polite—smiles in the hallway, casual greetings—but the warmth was gone. Everyone seemed more concerned with protecting their own place in the company.

Whispers began to circulate about why Hanna was chosen to help prepare for the meeting instead of someone else. Jealousy slipped in, subtle but sharp. Before long, she noticed she was no longer part of the regular group chat. It felt as if another conversation thread had sprung up somewhere else, one she wasn't invited to.

Robin eventually sent Hanna a text, casual on the surface but edged with curiosity:

> *Is your project going to call out individual store performance histories?*
> *Is my store on the list?*

Hanna didn't have the answer. She only knew the few details she'd been told, and those weren't much.

Robin wasn't just asking Hanna though. Quietly, she was texting other store managers, planting the same question in each of their minds: Was their store going to be singled out? Would the meeting expose who was underperforming? Soon those managers began to press Hanna as well, each trying to read between the lines. Anxiety spread quickly, and no one wanted to be the one caught off guard.

One afternoon in the break room, Robin remarked with a shrug,

"She's new. And so is Brad. What makes them think what worked at their old companies will work here? ZinkaTech isn't like those places."

No one challenged her, but the silence was its own kind of agreement. Robin kept at it in private conversations, sometimes with a smile, sometimes with a shake of her head, always with the same message: Be careful. Don't get too comfortable with these changes.

Finally, she decided to go higher. A few days before the meeting, she asked Karen if she could stop by her office. Karen agreed, though the timing couldn't have been worse—her own anxieties about the photo were still fresh, still gnawing.

Robin closed the door behind her and sat across from Karen's desk.

"I'm worried," she said plainly. "This whole setup with Janis and Brad... it feels rushed. Hanna's nice, but she doesn't have the history here. None of them do. And now we're supposed to let them stand up in front of everyone and dictate the future of our stores?"

Karen kept her expression neutral.

"They're not dictating, Robin. They're presenting. There's a difference."

Robin leaned forward.

"But what if it turns into more than that? What if this is the start of people getting replaced, shuffled around, cut out?"

She hesitated, then pressed further:

"Some of us have been talking. What would happen if we didn't show up to the meeting? If we—" she paused, "—boycotted?"

That word sent a chill through Karen. She sat up straighter, her voice firm but not harsh.

"Robin, that's not the path you want to take. You have concerns? Fine. Air them. Ask the tough questions. Challenge the direction if you think it doesn't fit.

But do it with reasons and genuine concern, not by walking out. A boycott would only hurt you, not them."

Robin frowned, considering her words.

Karen leaned in slightly, tone softening.

"You've been here a long time. You know the company. You've earned the right to ask questions. But if you refuse to even listen, you'll lose that voice. Don't throw away your influence."

For once, Robin stayed quiet. She tightened her lips to prepare her response. "I hear you. I'll think about it."

But as she left Karen's office, her mind was already moving. The boycott idea was dead, but her role as the voice of doubt was alive and well. If Janis wanted to lead, she would face questions—and resistance—from all directions.

Brad and Janis had no problem proving themselves. They had anticipated the rising tension and prepared for what was coming: sharper accountability, open ownership of poor scores, and honest confrontation with performance gaps. Once inside the meeting, there would be nowhere to hide—but that wasn't the point.

Their meeting had a different title—Grace. And they intended to live up to it. They planned to be the first to extend it, setting an example for other leaders who, for too long, had ruled their teams with fear.

Leaders who had driven performance into the ground by neglecting their people, leaving relationships to wither and unity to dissolve.

THE MEETING

The hallway outside the conference room pulsed with a strange kind of energy—half excitement, half unease. These were the same leaders who had met countless times before, but never outside headquarters. The change of setting made everything feel unsteady, as if the floor itself might shift. Familiar faces passed with quick nods and cautious smiles, the kind exchanged by people unsure whether today would bring celebration, reckoning, or both.

"Your seasonal setup done yet?" someone asked as they stepped aside to let another pass.

"Almost—still wrestling with the displays and that price change list they sent."

"You'll get it. How's your wife doing?"

"She's good—thanks for asking. Said to tell you she still uses that recipe you gave her."

The door to the conference room opened, letting out a faint ribbon of low jazz, smooth, almost hypnotic. Conversations quieted, just enough for the music to fill the space.

The room had been prepared with intention. Round tables draped in white cloths dotted the space, each set with water bottles, notebooks, and pens. The scent of coffee carried through the air, mingling with a quiet anticipation.

Chuck slipped into a chair across the room from Karen, leaving a deliberate gap. His fingers drummed lightly on the table, a rhythm meant to steady nerves he couldn't otherwise hide. Not too close, he thought. Let's not do anything to fuel the rumors.

Robin moved through the room, noting the quick nods, the subtle gestures, the whispered greetings. I hope they don't single out my store, she thought. But if they do, I'm ready. She eased into a seat near the back, keeping low, trying not to be noticed. Every movement was deliberate. Every glance sharp, scanning for openings. She was ready—ready to push back the moment Janis mentioned her store.

David and Karen exchanged brief, measured greetings as they took their seats. The unspoken tension around the photo lingered like a shadow between them, but for now, professionalism held the upper hand.

The soft laughter faded as the last attendees found their places. Hanna slipped quietly to her table, sensing the subtle shift in the room. Eyes lingered too long, whispers carried just far enough. They're expecting me to fail, she thought, tightening her posture ever so slightly. That's not my style. They'll see. She settled into her seat, her calm exterior masking the tension beneath, ready to meet whatever came next.

Brad stood near the front, eyes scanning the room with calm resolve. He knew the stakes. They all did. Janis entered last, her presence immediately drawing a collective stillness. She moved with quiet confidence to the front, pausing briefly to let the weight of the moment settle over everyone. The sign on the door had said only one word: Grace. It had been enough to bring them here. Enough to make them wonder.

She let her eyes move slowly across the room, catching glances, not holding them, as though she was measuring the light on the faces before her. Then she smiled—just enough for them to notice—but not so much that it gave anything away.

"When you hear the word grace," she began, gesturing briefly toward Brad and Hanna as she spoke, "most people think of kindness. Some think of forgiveness. A few think of elegance. And they're not wrong. But grace, in the life of an organization, is more than a virtue. It's a power source. The quiet engine that moves people toward their best... without forcing them there."

Her voice stayed even, warm.

"And yet," she continued, "the opposite is just as real. Graceless thinking. Graceless habits. They start so small—an assumption here, a quick dismissal there— and before long, they shape the air we all breathe. They shape how we speak, how we decide, how we work." She stepped closer to the edge of the table nearest her, hands open at her sides, palms relaxed.

"The goal today is to give a general overview of grace in action first, so we can see how it shows up in the work we do together. Then, we'll wrap things up with The Grace Grid and the Nine Signs of Graceful Leadership—markers that show grace fully realized. That's where the patterns we've been discussing will come to life."

A few moments passed as the words settled in. Then, from the back,

Robin spoke up quietly but clearly, "Janis, I've never really thought about grace like that before. I always thought it was just kindness or forgiveness... something gentle."

Janis turned toward her, eyes warm and steady.

"That's a common thought, Robin," she said softly. "But I'm talking about the kind of grace you can see in motion—the way a prize stallion runs, muscles flowing with power and ease; the way the best golfers swing, every movement precise and intentional; the way elite swimmers cut through water, strong and fluid at once. Grace in performance isn't softness. It's power, precision, and beauty moving as one. And when a team has that grace, you feel it before you can measure it."

Robin's hands, previously clenched at her sides, relaxed. Her usual edge softened as she processed the words, realizing the force behind them wasn't a threat —it was a standard to rise to. She nodded slowly, a quiet understanding settling on her face.

"That kind of grace... that's what we need," she said, her voice quieter than usual but resolute.

Janis smiled, a spark of hope in her eyes. "And that's why we're here—to choose grace together, not as a word, but as the way we lead, work, and build something stronger."

The room shifted just slightly, the promise of possibility stirring in the air. Brad leaned forward in his chair, his eyes still on Janis. He'd been locked in on every word, and now, he caught something subtle—a faint pause in her breath, the kind that comes when the mind is steady but the body is tired. He rose slowly, not to interrupt, but to carry her words forward without breaking their momentum.

"What Janis is talking about," he began, his voice low and steady, "isn't just an idea we nod along to. It's a call to action. And if we're going to choose grace, we can't just talk about it—we have to do something with it. Today."

He stepped toward the center of the room, making sure his eyes met the faces around the tables.

"That means pulling together as a team. Not just in spirit, but in action. One store at a time.

One challenge at a time. Together, until every location is strong enough to stand on its own—and then stronger still. And we're not putting this off. Pull out your calendars. We set the date for our first store visit now, before we leave this room. No wasted time."

As people reached for their devices, Brad pressed in. "When I say we're going to help, I mean really help. We're going to roll up our sleeves—wipe the dust from the products, straighten every shelf, organize every aisle so the store feels alive again. We'll finish the price changes that have been hanging out there for weeks, set up the seasonal displays still sitting in the back, and make sure the signs match the vision we want customers to see. We're going to leave each place better than we found it—every single time."

He let the image hang in the air before leaning in slightly. "We're still a young company, and right now, we're like a child—full of potential, but in desperate need of care, guidance, and protection. That's our job. To show up. To support. To fight for each other's success, because the truth is, we only rise if we rise together."

Brad paused just long enough for the weight of the moment to settle. "That's what grace looks like in action," he said. "And real grace isn't rushing in to rescue without giving people the dignity to try first. It's more graceful to give a leader the chance to lead their own store back to health before we make moves that interrupt lives or replace them. Grace gives room for growth before it takes drastic action. It trusts first, intervenes second."

He looked around one last time, then clicked to the first slide:

Leading Through Change

"Here's the thing about change—it's never neutral. It can go either way—better or worse. The change we're after is for the better: growth, improvement, evolution, survival. Because if you're not growing, you're dying. Just like a plant with no water, no sunlight, no nutrients—it withers away. Slowly at first... then all at once."

He paused. "So today, I'm challenging every leader here to grow. I'm challenging every person on this team to grow. I'm challenging every store we operate to grow—so that our customers will grow to love us again. So they'll give us back the grace they once had for us. So they'll trust us again—with their business, their loyalty, and their excitement about what's next."

He rested a hand on the podium. "Here's something we don't talk about enough: customers already give us grace. They give it to every company they do business with—even when that company stumbles. Big brands have survived scandals, bad press, even massive data breaches. People stuck with them... for a while."

Hanna, seated toward the front, nodded. "But Brad," she said, "that grace doesn't last forever."

Brad gestured for her to continue.

"At some point," Hanna said, standing, "customers run out of patience. They stop giving you the benefit of the doubt. They start avoiding your brand and find competitors to fill the space you once filled in their lives. And when that happens, it's not just about losing sales—it's about losing trust. And trust is a thousand times harder to win back than it is to lose."

Brad took the floor again. "That's why grace isn't just a 'feel-good' word—it's a strategic advantage. We can't buy it, but we can earn it. And the same way we'll go into stores to lift up—not take over—we must approach our customers the same way. We meet them where they are, give them reasons to believe in us again, and prove, day after day, that we deserve their trust."

He turned toward Hanna with a small nod. "And that," he said, "is where she's going to take us next."

Hanna stepped forward, clicking to the next slide:

The Grace Factor in Customer Service

"Every phone call we answer, every aisle we straighten, every return we process—it's either building grace or spending it. And once the account is empty, there's no quick deposit to fill it again. Today, I'm going to walk you through exactly how we can protect and grow the grace our customers give us—through service that makes them feel seen, valued, and respected. Service that turns transactions into relationships. Service that makes them believe in us again."

Hanna took a measured step toward the room, her voice clear but calm, the kind that cut through distraction without ever needing to rise.

"Let's start with the truth," she said. "Grace is built in moments—not in policies, not in slogans, not in clever marketing campaigns. It's built in the three seconds a customer stands at a counter deciding whether they feel welcomed or dismissed. It's in the extra two minutes an associate spends walking a customer to the exact shelf instead of just pointing. It's in the tone of our voices when someone calls with a complaint—and the fact that we choose to solve the problem instead of just 'processing' it."

She let her words breathe before continuing.

"Grace is not a department. It's not something customer service 'handles.' Grace is a responsibility every single person here carries—whether you're in sales, stocking, management, or corporate. It's in how we treat the people who choose to do business with us... and in how we treat the people who work beside us."

Hanna tapped the slide changer, revealing a simple chart labeled **The Grace Bank**.

"This is how I want you to think about it: every interaction with a customer is either a deposit or a withdrawal. When we make deposits—through respect, attentiveness, honesty—we increase our balance. We build reserves for the moments when we inevitably make mistakes. But withdrawals happen too —when we ignore a customer, when we're too busy to listen, when our stores feel disorganized, when our tone is rushed or clipped. And here's the danger: too many withdrawals, and the account runs dry. Once that happens, it's not just hard to rebuild—it's almost impossible."

She glanced toward Brad, then back to the room. "Brad talked about visiting our stores to restore them to health. I want to challenge you to think of your customer interactions the same way. Every store visit we make isn't just about fixing what's broken on the shelves—it's about making sure the people inside those stores are equipped and motivated to protect the grace we've earned."

The slide shifted again—this time to a photo of a clean, vibrant store next to one that looked neglected and tired.

"Customers don't separate service from the environment. To them, the way your store looks is the way your store feels. If it feels neglected, they assume they'll be neglected. But if it feels cared for, they believe they'll be cared for too. That's why grace starts the moment they walk through the door—before we've even said a word."

She stepped closer to the tables. "So here's the challenge: in the next 30 days, I want every single leader in this room to walk into their store—not as the manager, but as the customer. I want you to see it the way they see it. The smells, the lighting, the cleanliness, the way your team greets them—or doesn't. And then I want you to make one tangible improvement every single day. Not a plan. Not a meeting. An action."

She paused, scanning the room to see pens scribbling notes. "Because grace isn't built in theory—it's built in the details we control every day. And when those details say, 'We see you, we value you, we respect you,' customers will give us something no competitor can buy: another chance."

Hanna clicked the remote, and the screen shifted. The jazz faded into the background of silence as two line graphs appeared—one jagged, full of sharp peaks and plunges, the other smooth, curving steadily upward.

She glanced toward Brad. "This is where you come in."

Brad stood, moving closer to the screen. He traced the smoother line with his hand, then turned back to the room.

"Grace doesn't live only in words or ideals. It shows up in the numbers, too. Think of any metric—sales, turnover, customer satisfaction, productivity—plotted on a line graph."

Brad continued. "When grace is present in execution, the line moves with rhythm: small rises and dips, steady adjustments, a kind of breathing pattern that shows refinement at work. Leaders are learning, adapting, and responding in ways that build trust and consistency."

He shifted his hand to the jagged line. "But when grace is absent, the line swings wildly—sharp spikes, deep drops, violent swings that signal instability. That kind of turbulence usually comes from one of three things."

He ticked them off with his fingers. "First, unrefined operations. This often isn't because people don't care, but because they haven't had the practice, role play, or coaching needed to master their skills. Processes remain clumsy because the team hasn't rehearsed enough to move with fluency."

Chuck leaned forward. "So you're saying the inconsistency isn't from laziness—it's from a lack of reps?"

Brad nodded. "Exactly. Think of it like a musician who's sight-reading every performance instead of practicing scales. The talent is there, but without repetition and refinement, the execution will always be shaky."

He moved on. "Second, unclear or inconsistent policies—rules that change with the wind."

Karen frowned slightly. "We've had that. One quarter the focus was all about upselling, then suddenly the priority shifted to speed at checkout. No wonder people felt whiplash."

Brad gave a small smile. "That's a perfect example. When the rules keep shifting, the line reflects chaos instead of growth."

He raised a third finger. "Third, a fractured culture —teams reacting emotionally instead of moving in rhythm."

Brad let the contrast hang on the screen before continuing. "Grace, then, isn't just a moral quality—it's a stabilizer. It doesn't remove change or challenge, but it keeps an organization from whiplash. You can see it in smoother curves, steadier progress, and the confidence that tomorrow's numbers won't undo today's gains."

Hanna raised her hand, gesturing toward the slide. "So what you're saying is, when the culture breaks down, even if the—"

A dull thump cut through the room. Heads turned. Janis was slumped forward, her cheek pressed against the round table. A coffee mug tipped over beside her, sending dark liquid pooling toward the edge.

"Janis!" Karen's voice cracked as she shot from her seat. She grabbed Janis's shoulder and shook gently.

"Janis, can you hear me?"

The room froze for half a heartbeat—then chaos moved in. Chairs scraped back. Someone gasped.

"I'm calling 911!" shouted Mark from the back, already fumbling for his phone.

"I'll get the first aid kit!" another voice called from near the door.

Brad and Hanna were suddenly at Janis's side.

"She's not breathing," Brad said, his face blanching. "Hanna, help me roll her."

They eased Janis to the carpeted floor. Brad's hands shook for just a second before he locked them over her chest and began compressions.

"One, two, three, four..." Hanna counted out loud, kneeling beside him.

Robin's voice cut in, steady but urgent. "Everyone, circle up. Pray. Right now."

Hands reached for hands, shoulders touched shoulders, and a circle formed around the scene—dozens of bowed heads, murmured prayers filling the air.

"Lord, touch her body," Robin prayed, voice breaking. "Bring her back to us. Give wisdom to these hands trying to save her."

The wail of sirens grew louder until it spilled into the building. Paramedics rushed in, setting down gear, voices clipped and professional.

"Clear space, please!" one of them ordered.

Brad stood back, chest heaving, sweat beading on his forehead. Hanna put a hand on his shoulder, but his eyes never left Janis. A defibrillator's pads were placed against her chest. A jolt, a pause—then a faint gasp.

"She's breathing," a paramedic confirmed. Relief swept the room in a rush—tears, sighs, whispered thank-yous.

They loaded Janis onto the stretcher. As the team wheeled her out, Brad followed until the paramedic gently stopped him.

"She's stable. We'll take good care of her," the medic said.

Brad just nodded, his jaw tight. "She's my friend. She's... she's more than that. She's the reason I still believe we can turn this place around."

Outside, the sun had shifted low, casting long shadows across the parking lot. One by one, the leaders walked to their cars, silent but united, following the ambulance to the hospital.

Hours later, they filled the hospital lobby—some pacing, others sitting with heads in hands. No one checked their phones. No one talked about sales numbers.

Brad sat apart, elbows on his knees, staring at the floor. Hanna came over and knelt in front of him.

"She's strong," Hanna said quietly. "She's got more fight in her than anyone I've ever met."

"I know," Brad said, his voice rough. "But I've seen too many good people... just go. I can't—" He stopped, swallowing hard. "I can't lose her."

Robin's voice carried softly across the room. "Whatever's going on in our stores doesn't matter right now. Not one bit. We've got something bigger to pray for."

Everyone nodded, a few more hands linked together. For that night, the only bottom line that mattered was Janis's heartbeat.

The hours in the hospital lobby felt longer than they were. The group stayed together, some sitting in clusters, others pacing the hallway. No one left—not for dinner, not for a phone call, not for anything. Brad sat near the window, his elbows on his knees, eyes fixed on nothing. Hanna stayed close, checking in with the nurses every so often, coming back with updates that were more about reassurance than new information.

When a nurse finally stepped into the lobby and called Brad's name, everyone turned.

"She's awake," the nurse said, a small smile breaking her professional calm. "You can come back—two at a time."

Brad was on his feet before she finished speaking. Hanna followed him down the quiet hallway, the sound of their footsteps soft against the polished floor.

They found Janis propped up in the hospital bed, pale but alert, a thin blanket pulled to her waist. An IV line ran to her arm. She looked at them, her voice soft but steady. "You two look like you've been through a war."

Brad didn't laugh. He stepped to her side, his hand gripping the rail. "You scared the life out of us, Janis."

Hanna moved closer. "Scared all of us," she said. "The whole team's out there. Haven't moved an inch since the ambulance pulled away."

Brad nodded toward the door. "They're still downstairs, Janis. Every last one of them. We told them the meeting's over for the day, but no one's going home. They just want to be here for you."

Her eyes welled instantly. "I don't want to be a burden on anyone. Not like this."

Brad's voice softened. "You're not a burden. You've carried us more times than you know. Let us carry you now."

For a moment, Janis pressed her lips together, fighting the tears, but they came anyway. "I don't even know what to say to that."

"You don't have to say anything," Hanna said gently. "Just rest. We'll tell them you're okay."

As they stepped toward the door, a nurse stopped them. "I've never seen anything like that group in the lobby," she said quietly. "We told the hospital director, and he'd like to offer them our upstairs conference

113

room for tomorrow, if you'll all be back. Said it was... inspiring. The way you all stayed together."

Brad managed a small smile. "They are inspiring."

When they returned to the lobby and shared the news, relief filled the room. Some laughed softly, others wiped away tears. Shoulders dropped, tension eased. For now, the stores, the numbers, the endless lists could wait.

Tonight, they had their friend. Tomorrow, they'd have a room upstairs. And maybe, in some way, they'd all leave this place stronger than when they walked in.

THE NEXT MORNING

B y sunrise, word had already spread through the hospital. Staff members who had been on other floors came by just to see "the team that never left." Someone posted a photo online of the group holding hands in prayer the night before, and within hours, Janis's story went viral. Social media lit up with comments from customers sharing memories of kindness from the team—moments they hadn't forgotten.

Inside the stores, something unexpected happened. Customers started showing up in larger numbers, not just to shop, but to talk about what they'd seen on the news. Shelves that had been slow to move for months were suddenly empty. "I came because I wanted to support people like that," one customer told a cashier.

The employees—who just days earlier were worried about sales quotas—found themselves recognized in the community. A barista at a coffee shop stopped a cashier and said, "Hey, you're one of the hospital people, right? That's amazing."

It was surreal. In a way, the crisis had done what no sales initiative or promotional campaign could—it made the team human in the eyes of their community. And being human turned out to be their greatest selling point.

And in that sudden flood of goodwill, Brad saw it clearly.

"This is grace," he told the group in the conference room. "Exactly what Janis has been talking about. People giving us another chance—not because of a coupon or a sale, but because they've seen our heart. They're looking past our mistakes and giving us room to grow again."

A knock at the door pulled every head toward the entrance. It opened slowly, and there she was—Janis—frail but standing, one hand resting lightly on the doorframe. The color hadn't fully returned to her face, but her eyes were clear, sharp, and unmistakably hers.

The room froze for half a beat before breaking into applause, not the polite kind but the raw, unplanned kind that bursts out when relief overwhelms you. Chairs scraped back as people stood, some clapping, some wiping at their eyes.

Brad was already moving toward her. "You're supposed to be resting," he said, though his smile gave him away.

"I am," Janis said with a small laugh, her voice a little thinner than usual. "Just... resting in the right place now."

Karen—seated between Chuck and David—rose and pulled out the empty chair beside her. She gave a small wave for Janis to come closer, and the team instinctively shifted, making space. Janis eased into the seat, and the three of them—Karen, Chuck, and David—closed in around her, not to crowd her but to keep her in their circle, as if proximity alone could shield her from anything else that might come.

For a few moments, no one spoke. It was enough just to have her there, in the same room, breathing the same air, still part of them.

Then Janis took a slow breath. "There's something you all need to know," she said, her voice steady despite the strain. "I was diagnosed with breast cancer weeks ago. I've been carrying it quietly, remembering my husband's fight with cancer, trying to stay strong for the work. But... I can't keep that from you anymore. I want you to know what I'm facing—and that I'm not giving up."

Karen's eyes brimmed as she bent forward and wrapped Janis in a hug—not the kind meant for sympathy, but the kind that remembered. The kind that reached back to their very first lunch together in Janis's first two weeks at the company, when they had shared stories and laughter before the pressures of work had crowded in.

When they separated, Brad spoke quietly. "You should know something. Word about you has traveled farther than we could've imagined. People are talking —about your fight, about this team, about the way we showed up for each other. And they're not just talking. They're feeling it. They're… giving us grace."

Janis looked around the table, her gaze lingering on each face. "Then let's not waste it," she said quietly.

The door to the conference room swung open, and a hospital liaison stepped in. "There's… quite a crowd outside," she said, almost hesitant. "News crews. People from the community. Signs. They're asking for Janis."

The team exchanged glances. It wasn't a question of whether to go—it was a question of how.

Karen was the first to stand. "Brad, Janis—you two should be up front. I'll stand with you," she said, her voice calm but firm. "The rest of us will be right behind you."

It was settled without debate. Chairs pushed back, jackets were straightened, and the group moved together as one—shoulder to shoulder, step for step— down the hall and toward the hospital's main entrance.

The automatic doors slid open, and sound rushed in. Applause. Shouts of encouragement. A patchwork of handmade signs filled the air—"Get Well Soon, Janis!" "We're With You!" "Janis, You Rock!"—held by neighbors, customers, and complete strangers.

Cameras pivoted as the group emerged, the afternoon sun catching the line of faces.

Brad and Karen flanked Janis at the front, the rest of the team fanning out behind them in a united wall. Janis stepped toward the cluster of microphones. She didn't need to raise her voice—silence fell the moment she began. "I wanted you to hear this from me," she said, her tone steady but intimate. "I have breast cancer. I've been living with the diagnosis for weeks now, remembering my husband's battle, trying to keep going without bringing this weight into our work. But today, I want to stand here, with my team, and tell you that I am ready to fight—alongside every man, woman, and child facing this disease."

The words hung in the air. The cameras caught everything—the determination in her eyes, the hand Karen kept lightly on her back, the quiet solidarity in the faces behind her.

It wasn't a sales pitch. It wasn't strategy. It was simply human truth, offered freely. And in that moment, the bond between Janis, her team, and the community became unshakable.

Within hours, the footage was everywhere—news broadcasts, social media feeds, even international outlets picking up the clip. Hashtags multiplied, messages poured in, and the image of Janis flanked by her team became a symbol far larger than their company. The story had moved beyond the walls of the hospital, beyond their own city. And as Brad scrolled through the flood of support that night, he realized this wasn't just a moment—they were in the middle of something that could change everything.

The first scheduled store visit came just days later. True to their word, the entire leadership team—board members included—showed up at the Grand Rapids location before the doors opened. No one stood on the sidelines. Jackets came off, sleeves rolled up.

They moved through the store with a quiet determination, each task aimed at eliminating one of the five poisons Janis had warned them about.

Indifference was the first to go. Shelves were straightened, dust wiped away, and displays refreshed until the space looked cared for again.

Assumptions fell next. Price tags were checked and updated one by one, old signage replaced with clean, bold displays—making sure nothing was left to guesswork.

Disconnection was met with a handshake and a smile. Every customer who walked in was greeted with genuine eye contact, their names learned, their questions answered.

Avoidance had no place here. Orders were filled without delay, issues addressed on the spot instead of kicked down the road.

And **blame** never had a chance to surface—because everyone pitched in, no job too small, no corners cut.

As they straightened the back stockroom, Karen paused and took a breath. She turned to Janis, meeting her gaze.

"Janis... I need to say something," she began. "About the photo Brad asked me about. I blamed you in my mind—made you responsible for the stress I felt at work, at home. But the truth is... it wasn't you. It was me. I let my fears get out of control and things got weird. I was the one putting my family, my job, and even my own peace at risk."

Janis blinked, slightly surprised, then softened. "Karen..." she said gently, "thank you for saying that. It takes courage to see your own part and to forgive. I want you to know—you never had to carry that burden alone."

Karen exhaled, relief in her shoulders. "I forgive you, Janis. Not because you did anything wrong—but because I don't want this to come between us. You didn't cause my stress. That was me, and me alone."

Janis smiled, her voice calm and warm. "And I forgive you, Karen. Grace works both ways—it's giving and receiving. What matters is that we move forward together."

Karen returned a small, genuine smile, the tension between them finally easing. Around them, the team continued working, the hum of purposeful activity filling the store. By closing time, the store felt different —not just cleaner, but alive.

The next morning, they took it a step further. Word had gone out on social media: free hotdogs, pizza, and popcorn for anyone who stopped by. It wasn't a sale—it was an invitation. A chance to connect. And the community showed up.

From the moment the doors opened, the place was packed. Families lingered in the aisles, chatting with employees. Shoppers snapped photos with team members they recognized from the hospital news coverage. Some came with no intention to buy anything—they just wanted to be part of the story they'd seen unfold.

All day, the smell of popcorn drifted through the store, mingling with the sounds of conversation and laughter. What had begun as a work visit felt more like a celebration—of resilience, of community, and of the simple act of showing up together.

As the last customers drifted out and the team began sweeping up stray kernels and empty pizza boxes, Brad paused near the doorway. He looked around the store—at the warm conversations still happening between employees, at the shelves that looked as if they belonged to a brand-new business, at the pride in the faces of people who hadn't smiled like this in months.

Indifference had been replaced with care.

Assumptions with clarity.

Disconnection with connection.

Avoidance with action.

And blame with shared responsibility.

For the first time in a long time, he didn't just believe the store could turn around—he knew it already had.

THE GRACE GRID

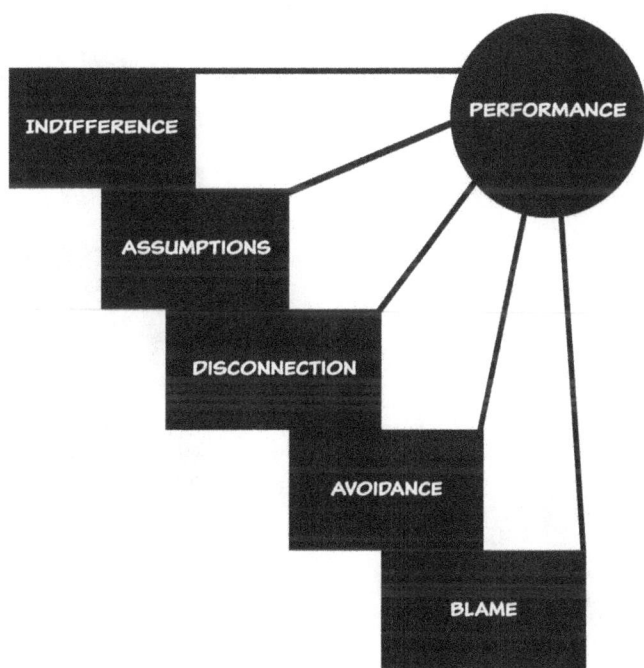

SETTING THE TONE

The conference table was crowded with coffee cups, notepads, and the lingering buzz from yesterday's packed store. Janis stood at the head, a remote in her hand, the first slide projected behind her.

"We'd planned to introduce this framework at our offsite meeting," she began with a small smile, "but as you know, circumstances cut that session short. Maybe that was for the best. After walking the floor with you yesterday, I think we're in a better place to see why this matters."

She clicked to the slide.

The screen filled with a staircase of five rectangles on the left, each carrying a word: Indifference. Assumptions. Disconnection. Avoidance. Blame. On the right sat a circle with a single word in the center: Performance. Five connecting lines stretched across, linking each step to the circle.

"These five aren't isolated issues—they're a grid," Janis said. "I call it the Grace Grid. Every time grace erodes in one of these areas, performance erodes right alongside it. When grace rises, so does performance." She traced the top step with her finger.

"Let's start with the first: Indifference. It's quiet, but it's corrosive. It's the slow erosion of care—for customers, employees, vendors, even the mission itself. When people stop noticing, they stop trying. And when they stop trying, results disappear. In Petoskey, for example, a seasonal display sat half-empty for weeks. The product was in stock, but no one felt responsible for keeping it full. Customers avoided it, and sales dropped."

Robin frowned. "So how do we know the difference between indifference and someone just being over-whelmed?"

"Good distinction," Janis said. "Overwhelmed people still care—they just can't keep up. Indifference is when caring itself disappears. For example, I've seen teams who were busy but still stopped to face customers with energy—that's being stretched, not indifferent. But I've also seen cashiers who didn't even look up when customers entered. That's indifference. Presence is the cure."

She moved to the next step.

"Assumptions are dangerous because they feel harmless. We assume customers know our value. We assume employees understand expectations. We assume managers are aligned. But assumptions create blind spots, and blind spots cost money. In Onaway, new hires were never shown half the store procedures because everyone assumed the training was happening."

Hanna tilted her head. "But aren't some assumptions natural? We can't explain everything all the time."

"True," Janis replied. "But in leadership, unchecked assumptions multiply. Take pricing tags—we assume they're accurate until a customer points out a mistake. By then, the damage is done. Or when managers assume their teams welcome new hires naturally, but instead the new person feels like an outsider and leaves. It's better to check twice than to assume once."

Her finger traced the third step.

"Disconnection is when people stop seeing the link between their work and the mission. They may be busy, but they're not aligned. In Detroit, shifts complete their tasks but don't communicate with the next one. It's like passing the baton without making eye contact."

Justin leaned forward. "So how do you spot disconnection before it becomes a crisis?"

"When good work doesn't add up to good results," Janis said. "For example, I walked into a store where merchandising was beautiful, but promotions weren't being communicated. The result? Slow sales, even though the team worked hard. Disconnection wastes effort. The cure is alignment—helping every role see how their work ties to the win."

She tapped the fourth step.

"Avoidance is stepping around problems instead of through them. It may feel like diplomacy, but in the long run, it poisons results. A store once left a pricing error uncorrected for a week because no one wanted to upset the vendor. That hesitation cost sales."

Brad raised a hand. "But isn't some avoidance healthy? Protecting relationships, for example?"

"Not when it sacrifices truth," Janis said. "I've seen leaders avoid giving performance feedback because they didn't want conflict. But the rest of the team saw the problem every day, and morale tanked. Protecting one person's feelings hurt everyone else. Facing issues quickly is the only real protection."

Finally, she rested her hand on the last step.

"Blame is the easiest way to feel right and the fastest way to lose. It shifts responsibility away from the person who can fix the problem and turns every challenge into a stalemate. Two departments at one store spent days pointing fingers over an ordering error, while customers walked out empty-handed."

Karen leaned in. "But how do you stop blame without sounding like you're blaming people for blaming?"

Janis smiled. "By shifting focus. In one store, instead of debating whose system failed, the manager asked, 'What's the fastest way we can get product on the shelf today?' Ownership moved the team forward, and customers got what they needed. That's the alternative to blame."

She stepped back, letting the whole grid fill their vision. "These five steps are not theory. They're mechanics. Grace fuels performance. Performance reveals grace. They rise and fall together."

The room was quiet for a moment, each person taking in the full grid. Eyes traveled from step to circle, then back again. Some nodded slowly, others scribbled notes, the weight of the connections settling in.

Karen leaned back in her chair, folding her arms, a small smile touching her lips. Finally, it makes sense, she thought. All those little frustrations, all those missteps—they weren't random. They were signs we could act on. Signs that grace and performance really do rise and fall together.

Brad exhaled, running a hand through his hair. "This... changes how I see the stores," he muttered, mostly to himself, but loud enough for a few to catch it.

Janis let the pause stretch just long enough before she spoke again. "Tomorrow, when we're in Detroit, watch for these steps in action. See where grace is missing, and step in. Every action, every conversation, every decision—it all matters."

The team exchanged glances, some with quiet determination, others with the kind of reflective focus that comes when insight finally clicks. The Grace Grid wasn't just a slide on a screen. It was a map. A way forward. The silence broke when David leaned forward, his brow furrowed.

"Janis, all this makes sense," he said, "but how do we know if we're actually leading with grace? I mean... what does it look like in practice, day to day?"

"That's the right question," Janis replied. "The Grid shows you where performance erodes. But there are also signs—habits of leadership—that tell you grace is present. I call them the Nine Signs of Graceful Leadership."

She clicked, and the slide shifted: nine short phrases arranged like guideposts, each with a question beneath it.

Chuck gave a low whistle. "Nine, huh? Sounds like we've got homework."

Janis smiled. "Maybe. But these aren't rules to memorize—they're mirrors. They reflect back whether you're leading with grace or without it."

Carl, the younger manager from Robin's store, squinted at the first phrase.

Trust Talent, Don't Contain It

"So this means what—just letting people do whatever they want?"

"Not quite," Janis said. "It means we hire people for their strengths, then give them room to use them. For example, one of your cashiers was sketching new endcap designs on her break. Instead of ignoring it, what if we encouraged that creativity? Grace creates space for talent to grow, instead of squeezing it into old molds."

Robin shot Carl a sideways glance, half amused. "That sound familiar?"

Carl chuckled sheepishly. "Okay, fair point."

Hanna tapped her pen on the second sign.

Listen to Learn, Not to Respond

"I'm guilty here," she admitted. "Half the time in meetings, I'm just waiting for my turn to jump in."

"Most of us are," Janis said. "But listening with curiosity—not defense—unlocks ideas. Yesterday in Detroit, one stock associate quietly suggested a fix for our late deliveries. No one had asked him before. When leaders listen like learners, they find hidden solutions."

David raised his hand slightly, still studying the list.

Learn from Departures

"You're saying we should actually celebrate when people quit?"

"Not celebrate," Janis said gently. "But notice. Every departure teaches something. Was the culture unsustainable? Was leadership inattentive? Even quiet resignations are feedback. If we ignore those lessons, we'll repeat the same mistakes."

Brad leaned in. "I like this one—*Watch How New Hires Are Treated*. We're terrible at that. Sometimes they're left standing around, not sure what to do."

"Exactly," Janis said. "The way a culture welcomes newcomers reveals whether grace is present. Think of their first month as a fragile bridge. Do we guide them across, or let them stumble?"

The group nodded, a little more sober now.

Then Chuck, arms crossed, pointed to another.

Model Calm in Chaos

"Janis, that's easier said than done," he countered. "When everything's on fire, how do you not panic?"

"Calm is contagious," she answered. "In one storm last year, the best leader I saw didn't have all the answers. But he stood steady, listened carefully, and said, 'We'll find a way through.' His calm gave the team enough courage to keep moving."

Karen glanced up at the next sign, reading it softly.

Celebrate Others First

She tilted her head toward Robin. "You're good at this. Always deflecting credit."

Robin shrugged. "Not always. But I've noticed when I celebrate someone else, the team pulls tighter. Feels different."

"Exactly," Janis said. "Grace doesn't hoard the spotlight—it shares it. The loudest applause should never be for ourselves."

Carl, still flipping pages in his notes, looked at the seventh:

Correct Without Crushing

"This one hits home," he muttered. "I once quit a job because a manager tore me apart in front of everyone."

Several heads nodded around the table.

"Accountability should never require humiliation," Janis said firmly. "Correction can be strong and still preserve dignity. Done well, people walk away stronger, not smaller."

David tapped the eighth sign.

Choose the Long View

"Feels like the hardest one in retail. Everyone's

chasing numbers this quarter."

"That's the trap," Janis replied. "Short wins are like sugar—they spike, then crash. Grace plants seeds: trust, empowerment, culture. Those are harder, but they last."

Finally, Chuck leaned back in his chair, reading the last sign aloud.

Teach by Example

He let the words hang, then smirked. "So if my team imitated me in everything... yikes."

The room laughed, breaking some of the heaviness.

"That's why it matters," Janis said, her voice steady but kind. "Culture is contagious. Your example is the most powerful teacher you'll ever be."

The group grew quiet again, the nine signs glowing on the screen behind her.

Brad exhaled. "So the Grid shows where we're breaking down. And these signs... they show us what to practice instead."

"Exactly," Janis said. "The Grid diagnoses. The Nine Signs lead us forward."

DETROIT

The Detroit store buzzed as the leadership team filed in behind Janis. She paused at the threshold, clipboard tucked under her arm.

"Today we're watching for patterns," she said. "Indifference, assumptions, disconnection, avoidance, blame. See them, address them, and focus on solutions."

Karen fell into step beside her, matching her pace as they moved down the main aisle.

"No engagement, no rhythm. Their files are almost empty.," she said. "Could be a good thing, but it's not. They're skipping the process—no documentation at all, just hirings and termination letters. People disappear before they ever get a chance to develop."

Janis tilted her head. "Tell me—who have these managers promoted in the last decade?"

Karen blinked. "Promoted?"

"It's the first question I ask when I want to know if a team is alive," Janis said softly. "A living team passes on strength. A dead team hoards it. No pulse means no growth."

Karen frowned, following Janis's gaze toward the managers clustered near the service desk.

"You think this is about self-preservation?"

"Sometimes," Janis said. "When leaders won't coach, it isn't always laziness. It can be fear. If they elevate someone, that person might surpass them. Better to prune talent early than risk being replaced. It's a terrible kind of math—short-term safety that guarantees long-term collapse."

As they moved down the electronics aisle, Janis noticed Juan stacking printer cables without glancing at the waiting customer. She stepped closer.

"Juan. Look at her. Just greet her."

Startled, he smiled tentatively. "Hi, can I help you?"

The customer's face brightened. Within moments, she had the wireless speaker she wanted, and Juan's shoulders eased, as if he'd been granted permission to exist differently. Janis turned back to the group.

"See? Not laziness. Not even indifference. It's the absence of safety. When people believe mistakes erase them, they stop trying. Coaching restores courage. Grace reopens the path."

Passing printing services, Janis slid aside a pallet of toner blocking the kiosk.

"This isn't about tasks—it's about signals. If no one shows you that details matter, you assume they don't. Coaching is what tells people where to look. Grace is what gives them space to practice noticing."

At software and supplies, a hesitant customer asked where to find accounting programs. Bryan pointed vaguely, then drifted away. Janis called him back.

"Walk with them," she said. "To you, it's nothing. To them, it's everything. And when your shift ends, tell the next associate what happened. That's how the thread keeps going."

The managers exchanged uneasy glances. They hadn't lost control of tasks—they had lost pulse.

Carl smirked. "So, when we talk about pulse... are we talking vital signs? Should I get a stethoscope for the electronics aisle?"

Bryan laughed. "Or check the pulse at checkout—if it's high, maybe you take a break. If it's low... greet more customers!"

Laughter bubbled through the group. A couple of associates, overhearing, grinned and nudged each other.

One pressed two fingers to his wrist and called out, "Pulse is strong in paper aisle!"

Another chimed in from behind the counter, "Might need CPR in software!"

The floor lightened. For the first time, engagement wasn't forced—it was contagious.

Janis let the moment linger before folding it into a lesson. "Exactly," she said. "Pulse isn't just an analogy —it's energy, engagement, accountability. Awareness first, action second. When it dips, coaching—or a simple self-correcting action like greeting more customers—restores it. That's true accountability. You get the chance to self-correct before intervention. That's how teams stay alive."

Karen leaned in quietly. "That little joke—did you see how it pulled the associates in?"

Janis nodded. "That's leadership, too. Atmosphere and culture must always connect with company values. The leader on duty sets the atmosphere. If it's fear, the store shrinks. If it's possibility—even laughter —the store breathes again. It can't always be about correction, accountability, and discipline. A good leader knows how to create moments of joy, because fun is not the opposite of accountability. Fun is what makes accountability sustainable."

Karen looked back at the associates still chuckling. "So the laughter wasn't wasted."

"No," Janis said, watching the team with a small smile. "It was a sign of life."

The next day the store carried the same energy as Grand Rapids had just days earlier. Hotdogs, popcorn, and pizza filled the air with the scent of community.

Families lingered in the aisles, chatting with employees who had become familiar faces from the media coverage. The store wasn't just a place to shop anymore—it was a gathering point, a celebration of resilience and care.

From Detroit, the team continued their tour, store by store, carrying the momentum. Each location followed the same approach: clean, organize, engage, and coach. Customers responded, not just to the products, but to the human connection.

THE LAST APPOINTMENT

The exam room felt both familiar and foreign. Janis had sat in this chair before, her hands folded in her lap, her eyes on the same white walls. But this time, the weight in her chest wasn't dread—it was the heavy, fragile hope that maybe, finally, this would be over.

Dr. Gannenburg entered quietly, a folder tucked under her arm. Her expression was calm but unreadable, and Janis found herself searching for clues in the way the doctor's mouth held its shape, in the way her steps measured the space between the door and the stool.

"Janis," Dr. Gannenburg greeted warmly, taking a seat. "How are you feeling today?"

Janis tried a small smile. "Like someone waiting for the rest of the story."

The doctor chuckled softly, glancing down at the closed folder on her lap. "Fair enough." She rested her hands on top of it, her fingers tapping once, then stilling. "I have your scans and labs here. Before I say anything, I want to tell you—whatever the words are that come next—you have done extraordinarily well. You've walked this road with courage, discipline, and a kind of hope that... well, not everyone can summon."

Janis swallowed, her gaze locked on the edge of the folder. "That sounds like you're preparing me for bad news."

"Not bad," the doctor said, her voice gentle. "But I want you to understand how much this moment matters."

She flipped the folder open, scanning the top page, then the second. The room seemed to shrink around them, each turn of the page a drumbeat in Janis's chest.

Janis leaned forward slightly. "Please—just tell me."

Dr. Gannenburg looked up, her eyes meeting Janis's squarely. "There is no sign of cancer. None. Your scans are clear. You are cancer-free."

The words seemed to hover in the air for a heartbeat before sinking in. Janis's hand flew to her mouth, the breath she'd been holding rushing out all at once. Her eyes blurred with tears.

"You're sure?" she asked, almost afraid to believe it.

The doctor smiled now—broad, certain. "I am sure. The treatments worked. Your body responded beautifully. And unless something changes, we'll only see each other for routine checkups from here on out."

Janis's shoulders sagged with relief. She laughed through her tears. "I don't even know what to say."

"You don't have to say anything," Dr. Gannenburg replied, reaching across to squeeze her hand. "Just keep living the way you've been living—fully, fiercely, and without apology."

For a moment, neither spoke. Janis thought of Jacob, of all the nights she had sat in rooms like this holding his hand. She thought of the team waiting outside, of the commercials, of the billboards that would now carry not just a leader's face, but a survivor's.

Finally, she whispered, "I wish he could see this day."

The doctor's smile softened. "I think he can."

A NEW ROUTINE

The drive home from her final appointment felt unreal. Janis kept glancing at the road signs, half-expecting them to rearrange into some hidden message about what had just happened. She had heard the words—cancer-free—but now, behind the wheel, it felt like more than a diagnosis. It was a challenge.

For months her days had been shaped by appointments, treatments, scans, and recovery schedules. Now, all of that had been stripped away, leaving space. The question was: how would she fill it?

On instinct, instead of turning toward home, she pulled into a neighborhood grocery store. Inside, she lingered in the produce section. Bright greens, reds, yellows—all bursting with life. She filled her cart with vegetables, berries, apples, and citrus. She added nuts, seeds, whole grains. As she moved down the aisles, she wasn't chasing a diet trend or a guarantee. She was simply choosing life—

foods to nourish and strengthen, a small daily way to care for the body that had carried her through.

That evening, her kitchen looked different. The blender whirred to life as she made her first smoothie: strawberries, fresh spinach, half an avocado, pomegranate juice, a squeeze of lemon, half a banana, a drizzle of honey, and a few cubes of ice. The flavor was rich, tangy, and unexpectedly refreshing. She sipped it slowly, smiling at the sharp sweetness, tasting possibility in every gulp.

With it she prepared a simple meal: roasted vegetables and grilled fish, a pitcher of water always within reach. After dinner, she sat at the kitchen table with a notebook and sketched a plan:

> *Morning walks to start the day with movement.*
> *Some fresh daylight each day.*
> *Strength training twice a week—nothing extreme.*
> *Yoga on the weekends to stretch and breathe.*
> *Reconnect body and spirit.*
> *Daily hydration and rest.*

It wasn't about control, it was about stewardship. For the first time in a long time, she felt authority over her own body, not as a patient but as a participant.

When she closed the notebook, she set her glass of water on the nightstand and lay down. Sleep came easier than it had in months, carrying her not into dread but into tomorrow.

In the weeks that followed, the company expanded its message. Ads shifted in tone, no longer spotlighting items on shelves but instead showcasing people—employees laughing with families, small moments of care between team members and customers, the joy of simply being present together.

This time, Janis appeared in several spots herself. Not as a spokesperson reading lines, but as a survivor, a leader, and a symbol of resilience. She spoke briefly, sharing fragments of her story and reminding viewers that behind every purchase, behind every store, are people navigating real battles—and that care matters.

At the same time, the company launched a set of sustainability initiatives, reinforcing its commitment to care on a larger scale. Recycling programs, eco-friendly packaging, and local partnerships signaled that growth wasn't just financial—it was social, communal, and environmental. The company was learning to lead with responsibility and purpose.

Finally, the day came when Janis stood at the edge of the freeway, looking up at the new billboards. She wore the company polo, the pink cancer-free pin proudly fastened over her heart. Cameras captured her smile, the message clear: hope, resilience, and human connection had carried the day.

This wasn't just a marketing campaign—it was a celebration of people, of triumph over adversity, and of a company that had learned to lead with care and grace.

The momentum was unstoppable. The stores thrived, employees were engaged, customers returned in droves, and the culture—once vulnerable to the five patterns—was becoming one defined by presence, alignment, accountability, courage, and ownership.

Janis had not only faced her battle; she had helped shape a blueprint for sustainable, grace-centered leadership.

A NEW BEGINNING

Two years later, ZinkaTech had proven its strategy: acquire, restore, and grow with grace at the center. QB-KOZE was thriving, its turnaround a model for what could be achieved. And now, ZinkaTech had taken another bold step—acquiring a struggling retail chain that bore the same fractures QB-KOZE once carried.

The boardroom reflected that history. At the head sat Brad, now Chairman of the Board, steady and observant. Around the table were ZinkaTech's directors, the revitalized leaders of QB-KOZE, and the anxious executives of the newly acquired company. Past victories, present responsibilities, and future hopes gathered in one place. Janis stood before them —no longer the advisor in the shadows, but CEO, carrying the weight of leadership with confidence.

"Grace," she began, "is the glue that holds organizations together. Not just in moments of success, but especially in seasons of doubt, fatigue, and loss.

Grace binds people when incentives run out, when strategies falter, when strength alone isn't enough. It is the difference between organizations that collapse under pressure and those that rise above it."

Her words carried a stillness across the room. Some nodded slowly, remembering. Others leaned forward, as if hearing it for the first time.

Janis let the silence linger, then shifted slightly, her expression softening.

"And today, I want to introduce you to someone who has lived that truth. This is Hanna. Many of you know her work. She began at QB-KOZE during its most difficult days, when the company was tired, skeptical, and afraid. She helped lead teams through doubt, held space for their questions, and modeled resilience when answers weren't easy to find. Hanna is proof that grace isn't just theory—it's practice. She will carry this message forward as my advisor, and I can't imagine a more capable voice for this moment."

Hanna stepped forward, steady and assured. She glanced across the room—at Brad, at Janis, at the new leaders waiting for hope to feel real.

"I've been asked many times what grace really means," Hanna said. "To me, grace is simple: it's creating space. Space for people to fail without being discarded. Space for leaders to learn without shame. Space for organizations to stretch, stumble, and still move forward. Grace is not softness. Grace is strength that makes room—for people, for growth, for the future."

RESOURCES FOR GRACE-CENTERED LEADERSHIP

This section is designed to give leaders practical tools, exercises, and frameworks to apply grace intentionally in the workplace. Every resource connects directly to the five destructive behaviors that erode performance—Indifference, Assumptions, Disconnection, Avoidance, and Blame—and their grace-centered alternatives—Presence, Alignment, Accountability, Courage, and Ownership.

These resources are fully actionable. Leaders and teams can use them in meetings, one-on-ones, projects, or personal reflection. Each tool includes clear instructions, reflection questions, and examples so you can see how grace changes outcomes in real-life scenarios.

SECTION 1
TEAM PRACTICE TOOLS

Activities: Replacing Destructive Behaviors with Grace

Activity 1: Indifference → Presence

Scenario:
During a critical project, a key team member is quietly struggling while the rest of the team focuses on deadlines and meetings, unaware of the mounting pressure on their colleague.

Dialogue Prompts:
- What signals might we have noticed earlier that someone was struggling?
- How can leaders model presence in high-pressure situations?
- Have you ever witnessed or been part of "indifference" in a team? What happened?
- What could the outcome have been if presence had been applied here?

Facilitator Takeaways:
- Presence is not just physical attendance; it is noticing, listening, and responding with genuine engagement.
- Small actions of engagement prevent larger problems from developing.
- Presence builds trust, connection, and accountability within teams.

Examples of Presence in Action:
- Pausing to ask a colleague how they are managing a challenging workload.
- Giving full attention in meetings, avoiding phones and multitasking.
- Offering brief but meaningful acknowledgment of someone's contributions.

Activity 2: Assumptions → Alignment

Scenario:

Two departments are working toward a shared goal but have very different interpretations of priorities. Confusion escalates, and progress slows.

Dialogue Prompts:
- What assumptions might have caused the misalignment?
- How can leaders create clarity and alignment quickly?
- Share a time when assumptions caused friction in your team. How was it resolved?

- What practical steps can prevent assumption-based conflicts in the future?

Facilitator Takeaways:
- Alignment begins with clarity and shared understanding.
- Asking questions openly prevents misinterpretation.
- Regular check-ins and transparent communication reduce costly assumptions.

Examples of Alignment in Action:
- Holding a brief cross-department meeting to clarify priorities.
- Restating goals in written form to ensure everyone shares the same understanding.
- Confirming responsibilities and expectations explicitly instead of assuming knowledge.

Activity 3: Disconnection → Accountability

Scenario:
A project misses its deadline, and no one steps forward to take responsibility. Blame circulates quietly between departments.

Dialogue Prompts:
- What keeps teams from being accountable in situations like this?
- How can leaders encourage ownership without micromanaging?

- Have you ever experienced a culture of disconnection? How did it affect results?
- What actions can a team take to restore accountability quickly?

Facilitator Takeaways:
- Accountability grows from clear expectations and empowered ownership.
- Connection and open dialogue reinforce responsibility.
- Teams that practice accountability thrive under pressure.

Examples of Accountability in Action:
- Instituting visible progress trackers for projects.
- Encouraging team members to report on their own progress without fear of criticism.
- Recognizing individuals who take ownership, even if the outcome is imperfect.

Activity 4: Avoidance → Courage

Scenario:
A team member notices an unethical practice but hesitates to speak up, fearing conflict or repercussions.

Dialogue Prompts:
- What stops people from confronting uncomfortable truths?
- How can leaders create an environment where courage is safe and rewarded?

- Share an example where avoidance created bigger problems. How could courage have changed the outcome?
- How do we balance speaking up with respect and tact?

Facilitator Takeaways:
- Courage is modeled from the top and supported through trust.
- Avoidance erodes culture; courage sustains it.
- Encouraging dialogue and feedback empowers teams to act ethically and decisively.

Examples of Courage in Action:
- Addressing performance issues privately but directly.
- Speaking up about process flaws or risks before they escalate.
- Recognizing and rewarding team members who confront difficult situations constructively.

Activity 5: Blame → Ownership

Scenario:
After a client complaint, a team spends hours discussing who is at fault instead of how to prevent the issue in the future.

Dialogue Prompts:
- How does blame affect team morale and performance

- What shifts when team members take ownership instead?
- Share a moment where ownership turned a negative into a positive.
- How can we create habits of ownership in everyday work?

Facilitator Takeaways:
- Ownership replaces blame with problem-solving energy.
- Teams that embrace ownership are resilient and proactive.
- Recognizing contribution, not fault, strengthens culture and outcomes.

Examples of Ownership in Action:
- Redirecting a post-mortem from fault-finding to solution design.
- Encouraging team members to propose actions they will take to prevent repeat issues.
- Publicly acknowledging individuals who take responsibility for challenges and improvements.

WORKSHEET 1
PRESENCE

- **Behavior:** Absence of Presence
- **Solution:** Show up fully—physically, mentally, and emotionally.
- **Team Activity:**
  - Discussion Starter: Think of a time this month when you were in the room but not fully present. How did it impact the team?
  - Scenario: Imagine a leader who constantly checks their phone during meetings. What message does this send?
  - Group Reflection: What specific practices could we adopt to create more presence in our culture (e.g., tech-free meetings, opening with focus moments)?
  - Action Step: Agree on one ritual that will anchor presence over the next 30 days.

WORKSHEET 2
ALIGNMENT

- **Behavior:** Misalignment on Goals & Values
- **Solution:** Create shared understanding and language.
- **Team Activity:**
  - Discussion Starter: When was the last time you thought you were aligned—only to discover later you weren't?
  - Scenario: The marketing team launches a campaign without consulting operations. Customers are excited, but stores cannot deliver. What broke down?
  - Group Reflection: Where do we experience alignment gaps between departments or priorities?
  - Action Step: Write down the one sentence that defines your team's purpose this quarter and share it aloud.

WORKSHEET 3
ACCOUNTABILITY

- **Behavior:** Lack of Accountability
- **Solution:** Foster ownership at every level.
- **Team Activity:**
  - Discussion Starter: What's harder—holding others accountable, or holding yourself accountable? Why?
  - Scenario: A project deadline is missed. Everyone points to someone else. How should the leader respond?
  - Group Reflection: Where does accountability break down most often: goals, deadlines, follow-through, or communication?
  - Action Step: Agree on one accountability practice to experiment with (e.g., shared scoreboard, check-in cadence).

WORKSHEET 4
COURAGE

- **Behavior:** Avoiding Hard Conversations
- **Solution:** Lead with courage and candor.
- **Team Activity:**
  - Discussion Starter: Think of the hardest conversation you avoided. What happened as a result?
  - Scenario: A high performer is toxic to the team. Do you confront them or look away? What's at stake?
  - Group Reflection: What conversations are currently being avoided? What might happen if avoidance continues?
  - Action Step: Each person names one conversation they commit to having this week.

WORKSHEET 5
OWNERSHIP

- **Behavior:** Lack of Ownership Thinking
- **Solution:** Act like owners, not renters.
- **Team Activity:**
  - Discussion Starter: What is the difference between being an owner of outcomes and being a renter of a role?
  - Scenario: A leader says, "That's not my job." What message does that send?
  - Group Reflection: Where do people think like renters instead of owners?
  - Action Step: Each leader identifies one way to model ownership more visibly.

SECTION 2
DIAGNOSTIC TOOLS

Diagnostic tools help leaders measure, observe, and reflect on the current state of their teams and their own behaviors. They provide a baseline for action, highlight blind spots, and make the connection between grace and performance tangible.

TEAM ASSESSMENT
GRACE-CENTERED
LEADERSHIP

The team assessment is designed to evaluate the collective behaviors of a leadership team or department. It focuses on the five behaviors (Presence, Alignment, Accountability, Courage, Ownership) and identifies where the team is strong and where attention is needed.

How It Works:
- Each leader rates the team as a whole, not individuals, using a 1–5 scale:
    - 1 = Never
    - 2 = Rarely
    - 3 = Sometimes
    - 4 = Usually
    - 5 = Always
- After scoring all behaviors, tally results to determine strengths and vulnerabilities.

Behavior 1: Presence

Statements to rate:

1. Leaders give undivided attention in meetings.
2. People show up prepared and engaged.
3. Team discussions feel focused, not distracted.
4. Leaders actively listen before responding.

Fix-It Focus:

- If scores are low, introduce rituals to anchor presence: tech-free meetings, opening with a moment of focus, check-ins to notice workload pressures.
- Encourage small but consistent actions, like greeting team members individually at the start of meetings.

Behavior 2: Alignment

Statements to rate:

1. Goals are clear and well-communicated.
2. Teams understand how their work connects to the bigger mission.
3. Different departments coordinate instead of working in silos.
4. Leaders use shared language around priorities.

Fix-It Focus:

- Simplify goals into one-page strategies.
- Schedule cross-team checkpoints.
- Create clarity rituals like weekly updates with purpose statements.

Behavior 3: Accountability

Statements to rate:

1. Deadlines are consistently met.
2. Leaders hold themselves to the same standards as others.
3. Team members call out when commitments aren't honored.
4. Results are tracked and shared openly.

Fix-It Focus:

- Establish visible scoreboards.
- Build peer accountability.
- Model "owning mistakes" openly.

Behavior 4: Courage

Statements to rate:

1. Leaders address problems quickly instead of avoiding them.
2. Honest feedback flows up, down, and sideways.
3. Difficult conversations lead to better performance.
4. The team encourages healthy debate without fear.

Fix-It Focus:

- Start with small feedback loops.
- Train on difficult conversations.
- Reward candor and constructive challenge.

Behavior 5: Ownership

Statements to rate:

1. Team members take responsibility beyond their job description.
2. People solve problems instead of waiting for someone else.
3. Leaders act with a long-term mindset, not quick fixes.
4. Everyone feels accountable for customer outcomes.

Fix-It Focus:

- Reinforce "we, not they" language.
- Empower decision-making at all levels.
- Model ownership from the top.

Scoring & Debrief:

- 16–20 points per behavior = Strong foundation; continue reinforcing.
- 10–15 points = Vulnerable; needs attention.
- Below 10 = At risk; urgent intervention required.

Team Reflection Questions:

- Which behavior scored lowest? Why?
- Where do we see this behavior showing up in real life?
- What one experiment can we try this quarter to improve?

INDIVIDUAL ASSESSMENT GRACE-CENTERED LEADERSHIP

The individual assessment helps leaders examine their own behaviors and identify personal growth opportunities. Self-awareness is critical: leaders often overestimate their own performance or avoid reflecting on patterns that undermine culture.

How It Works:
- Rate yourself on each statement using a 1–5 scale (1 = Never, 5 = Always).
- Be brutally honest; this is for self-growth.
- After scoring, identify your lowest area and pick one habit to change in the next 30 days.

Behavior 1: Presence
- I give others my full attention when they speak.
- I avoid multitasking in conversations or meetings.
- I come to meetings prepared, not distracted.
- I listen first, then respond.

Behavior 2: Alignment
- I connect my team's work to the bigger vision.
- I communicate goals in a clear, simple way.
- I prevent silos by collaborating across functions.
- My language reinforces shared direction, not personal agendas.

Behavior 3: Accountability
- I consistently meet my commitments.
- I abide by the same standard I expect from others.
- I own mistakes instead of deflecting blame.
- I track results and share them transparently.

Behavior 4: Courage
- I address performance issues directly, not avoid them.
- I give feedback honestly and respectfully.
- I invite feedback on my own leadership.
- I encourage debate and dissent when it helps the team.

Behavior 5: Ownership
- I solve problems without waiting to be asked.
- I take responsibility for outcomes beyond my job description.
- I make decisions with a long-term lens, not just quick wins.
- I use "we" language instead of "they."

Scoring & Reflection:
- 16–20 points = Personal strength; continue modeling.
- 10–15 points = Growth area; pick one new practice to build.
- Below 10 = Blind spot; ask others for feedback and take immediate steps.

Self-Reflection Questions:
- Which behavior is my strongest?
- Which one do I avoid most often?
- What is one small daily habit I can change to shift my lowest score?

SECTION 3: MEASURING GRACE IN YOUR ORGANIZATION

Grace-centered leadership is not abstract—it is practical, measurable, and impactful. Leaders often ask: "How do I know if grace is really working in my organization?" The answer lies in the metrics you already track—coupled with a deliberate focus on how behaviors, relationships, and decisions reflect grace.

The Business Case: How Grace Impacts Results
Grace is a multiplier of performance, not a distraction from it. Leaders who integrate grace see measurable impact in several areas:

- **Sales:**
    - Customers who feel respected and served with care buy more, return more often, and recommend the organization to others.

- Grace reduces hidden costs like customer churn and service complaints.
- **Profits:**
  - A culture of grace lowers turnover, reduces training waste, and minimizes rework caused by mistakes
  - Teams with high morale, proper support, and clarity make fewer costly errors.
- **Confidence and Competence:**
  - Graceful leaders build confidence in their teams through positive feedback, effective training, and meaningful face time.
  - Confident employees act consistently, improving both quality and reliability.

Key Insight: Grace is not "soft." It is a strategic advantage that strengthens both culture and financial performance.

Metrics That Reveal Grace

Leaders can monitor grace through existing organizational data. Key areas to track include:

- **Employee Engagement and Reviews:**
  - Do team members feel valued, supported, and heard?
  - Rising engagement scores often mirror increases in presence, clarity, and accountability.

- **Hiring and Retention Data:**
  - High turnover signals disconnection or lack of support.
  - Graceful leaders examine whether new hires are welcomed, trained effectively, and integrated into culture.
- **Customer Service Metrics:**
  - Complaints, feedback, and service scores reveal how pressure affects employees' ability to deliver grace.
  - Grace ensures that employees have the tools, training, and time to serve effectively.
- **Sales and Productivity Metrics:**
  - Slow growth or missed goals often hide root causes like unclear expectations or weak processes.
  - Grace focuses on identifying system gaps before assigning blame.
- **Quality and Error Rates:**
  - Mistakes are rarely about talent alone—they often result from time pressure, unclear roles, or insufficient resources.
  - Grace seeks to fix the system, not punish the individual.

The Grace Audit: A Leadership Exercise

The Grace Audit is a practical way to connect metrics with leadership behavior.

Step 1: Take a printout of your most recent organizational metrics. Include sales, service, retention, productivity, and quality.

Step 2: For each area, ask:

- Could we have acted with more presence or clarity?
- Was the issue related to avoidance, blame, or disconnection?
- What specific grace-centered action could have prevented or corrected this outcome?

Step 3: Capture insights in writing and discuss with your team. Encourage a culture of learning and improvement, not punishment.

Step 4: Identify one measurable change each quarter to increase grace in systems, service, or leadership practices.

Practical Steps to Measure and Grow Grace

- **Weekly Reflection in Leadership Meetings:**
  - Choose one key metric and ask: "Where does grace fit here?"
  - Discuss recent successes and areas where grace could have improved outcomes.
- **Service vs. Pressure Analysis:**
  - Identify where employees must choose between speed and quality.

- Adjust processes to protect both employee well-being and customer experience.
- **Feedback Inventory:**
  - Review the last month of feedback given to staff.
  - Ask: Was it corrective only, or did it also build confidence and reinforce positive behaviors?
- **Grace Growth Plan:**
  - Each leader commits to one actionable, measurable change that will strengthen grace in their area.
  - Track results over time, revisiting metrics and adjusting approaches.

Closing Thought

Grace is not an optional leadership trait—it is a multiplier for results. When woven into daily decision-making:

- Employees become more resilient and engaged.
- Customers feel valued, leading to loyalty and advocacy.
- Metrics improve in tangible ways—sales, retention, quality, and productivity.

The numbers will not just show if grace is present—they will show how much it is worth.

SECTION 4: THE GRACEFUL TURNAROUND PLAYBOOK

When a business struggles, the natural reflex is often to cut costs, demand more from overworked teams, or lean into fear-based urgency. These responses may create short-term results, but they rarely build sustainable performance. The Graceful Turnaround Playbook provides a structured, grace-centered approach to stabilize, recover, and rebuild.

Grace is not sentimentality or soft leadership. It is a disciplined, strategic choice that strengthens both people and performance. This playbook offers practical steps leaders can apply immediately, regardless of industry or size.

Step 1: Stop the Bleeding
A turnaround begins with focus and clarity. Identify quick wins that preserve cash flow and prevent further losses.

Actions:
- Cut unnecessary processes: Remove workflows that create friction, confusion, or wasted effort.
- Communicate openly: Be transparent with employees, customers, and stakeholders about the short-term plan.
- Simplify offerings: Focus on products or services that generate revenue reliably. Suspend low-performing lines temporarily.

Instructional Tip: Transparency builds trust even in uncertainty. Employees are more likely to commit when they understand the rationale behind decisions.

Step 2: Engage the Team

People respond to trust, clarity, and connection, not spreadsheets alone. Graceful leaders invest time in meaningful engagement.

Actions:
- Share the truth: Communicate the business reality honestly but constructively. Avoid sugarcoating.
- Recognize effort: Celebrate small wins and individual contributions to maintain morale.
- Create connection moments: One-on-one check-ins, brief team huddles, or casual conversations remind employees they matter.

Instructional Tip: Engagement here is not indulgence; it is strategic attention that keeps talent focused and aligned with recovery objectives.

Step 3: Reset the Customer Connection
Customers sense organizational stress immediately. Grace ensures positive, consistent experiences even in turbulent times.
Actions:
- Apologize quickly: Acknowledge service lapses honestly, and commit to correcting them.
- Add small gestures: Handwritten notes, follow-up calls, or personalized thank-you messages signal care.
- Rebuild credibility: Deliver consistent, reliable service to regain trust and loyalty.

Instructional Tip: Customer retention is often more valuable than short-term revenue gains. Graceful responses can turn setbacks into loyalty opportunities.

Step 4: Measure What Matters
Graceful leadership requires metrics beyond finance. Track leading indicators of grace to guide decisions:
- Resolution quality: How many customer complaints are handled with dignity?
- Employee coaching: Are employees supported and guided, or primarily corrected?
- Retention: Are top performers staying despite stress?
- Cultural health: Are destructive behaviors being replaced with presence, clarity, accountability, courage, and ownership?

Actions:
- Establish a grace dashboard: Combine financial metrics with people- and culture-based indicators for a balanced scorecard.
- Review weekly: Make grace metrics part of the leadership team's standing agenda.
- Act on trends: If turnover spikes, morale dips, or service falters, intervene quickly with transparent communication and corrective support.
- Share progress: Publish simplified updates for staff to show how collective effort is moving the needle.

Instructional Tip: Combine these with traditional metrics (revenue, sales, productivity) to create a holistic view of the organization's recovery trajectory.

Step 5: Create a Cycle of Adjustment
Turnarounds are rarely linear. Graceful leaders implement feedback loops, course corrections, and continuous improvement cycles.
Actions:
- Weekly check-ins: Review progress against goals and metrics.
- Honest reviews: Discuss what worked, what didn't, and why—without blame.
- Adjust strategies: Be willing to pivot quickly in response to data and employee feedback.

Instructional Tip: The key is to hold people accountable without humiliation while adjusting strategies without panic.

Step 6: Integrate the Five Behaviors of Grace
During the turnaround, leaders must actively replace destructive behaviors with grace-centered alternatives:

- Indifference → Presence: Stay attentive, listen actively, and support employees and customers alike.
- Assumptions → Alignment: Clarify goals, check understanding, and communicate openly.
- Disconnection → Accountability: Empower ownership of results while fostering relational responsibility.
- Avoidance → Courage: Address problems directly, model tough conversations, and act decisively.
- Blame → Ownership: Focus on solutions, teach responsibility, and cultivate proactive problem-solving.

Actions:
- Audit current behavior: Identify where destructive patterns show up in meetings, performance reviews, or customer interactions.
- Model visibly: Senior leaders must embody the five grace behaviors in their daily actions.
- Reinforce consistently: Use recognition, feedback, and coaching to encourage adoption across teams.

- Embed in systems: Align hiring, training, and performance metrics with the five behaviors.

Instructional Tip: Integrate these behaviors into daily routines, team meetings, and decision-making processes. Leadership consistency creates cultural change faster than any memo or policy.

Step 7: The Payoff of Grace
Applying grace in a turnaround does more than stabilize the business—it transforms it:

- Customers trust the brand again.
- Employees become advocates instead of survivors.
- Culture strengthens and hardens against future crises.
- Profitability and performance recover more sustainably.

Actions:

- Document wins: Collect stories, testimonials, and examples of grace in action from employees and customers.
- Share results: Communicate both financial recovery and cultural progress to stakeholders.
- Institutionalize practices: Formalize grace-driven processes so they endure beyond the turnaround.
- Expand vision: Use momentum to pursue growth opportunities.

Instructional Tip: Track both quantitative results (sales, retention, productivity) and qualitative indicators (morale, engagement, trust) to demonstrate the full impact of grace-driven leadership.

Reflection Exercise for Leaders

To embed grace into turnaround strategy, ask yourself and your leadership team:

1. Where have I allowed fear or urgency to override grace in past decisions?
2. Which behaviors are still holding the team back, and how will I model their alternatives?
3. What one action today can create momentum for both performance and culture?

By reflecting deliberately and acting consistently, leaders replace reactive management with purposeful, grace-centered leadership, turning crises into opportunities for sustainable growth.

SECTION 5: THE GRACE GRID: A PRACTICAL GUIDE FOR LEADERS

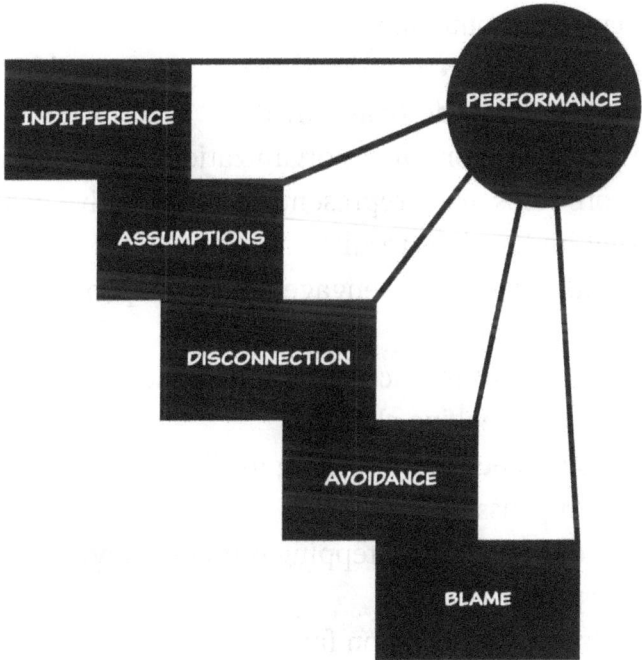

Introduction

The Grace Grid is a practical, step-by-step framework that allows leaders to connect behaviors, culture, and performance. It shows how grace and destructive behaviors rise and fall together, and provides a roadmap for replacing harmful habits with grace-centered alternatives.

Unlike abstract theories, the Grace Grid provides actionable insights that leaders can implement immediately to improve team performance, engagement, and customer outcomes.

Understanding the Grace Grid

The Grace Grid organizes organizational behavior into five core steps, each representing a destructive behavior that undermines results:

1. **Indifference** – disengagement from people, tasks, or outcomes.
2. **Assumptions** – acting on unverified beliefs instead of seeking clarity.
3. **Disconnection** – working in silos and losing sight of the mission.
4. **Avoidance** – sidestepping difficult conversations or problems.
5. **Blame** – focusing on fault rather than solutions.

These behaviors do not exist in isolation—they compound, pulling performance down like a cascading domino effect. Conversely, when each behavior is replaced with its grace-centered alternative, culture and performance improve:

- Indifference → **Presence**
- Assumptions → **Alignment**
- Disconnection → **Accountability**
- Avoidance → **Courage**
- Blame → **Ownership**

Step 1: Diagnose
Begin by assessing your organization across the five behaviors:
- Print or display the Grace Grid for your team.
- Walk through each behavior and ask:
  - Where do we see this happening in our organization?
  - What is the observable impact on performance, morale, and customer experience?
- Identify the behaviors that are dragging results down.

Instructional Tip: Encourage honesty and avoid finger-pointing. Focus on patterns, not individuals.

Step 2: Connect Behaviors to Performance
Each destructive behavior has a tangible cost:

- Indifference: Lost customer loyalty, disengaged employees, missed opportunities.
- Assumptions: Errors, inefficiencies, and repeated misunderstandings.
- Disconnection: Projects fall short, deadlines are missed, collaboration suffers.
- Avoidance: Problems grow, trust erodes, conflict festers.
- Blame: Innovation stalls, morale drops, teams fight internally rather than serving customers.

Instructional Tip: Use real examples from your organization. Illustrate how these behaviors have affected outcomes in the past.

Step 3: Replace Each Behavior with Grace
Presence over Indifference:
- Show up fully—physically, mentally, and emotionally.
- Actively notice and respond to teammates, clients, and processes.
- Small actions of engagement prevent larger issues.

Alignment over Assumptions:
- Clarify goals, expectations, and priorities.
- Ask questions openly to avoid misinterpretation.
- Use regular check-ins and transparent communication to reduce friction.

Accountability over Disconnection:
- Foster ownership at every level.

- Set clear expectations and empower decision-making.
- Encourage open dialogue about responsibilities and outcomes.

Courage over Avoidance:

- Address issues directly, honestly, and respectfully.
- Encourage team members to voice concerns and engage in constructive conflict.
- Model the courage you want to see in others.

Ownership over Blame:

- Encourage self-reflection and responsibility for results.
- Shift focus from fault to solutions.
- Reinforce proactive problem-solving.

Step 4: Measure Progress

Grace is visible in both qualitative and quantitative metrics:

- **Customer Satisfaction:** Are complaints handled respectfully? Do customers feel heard and valued?
- **Employee Engagement:** Are people staying, contributing, and demonstrating accountability?
- **Productivity and Quality:** Are deadlines met? Are errors reduced?
- **Conflict Resolution:** Are problems addressed constructively rather than avoided or blamed?

Instructional Tip: Track progress over time. Use a baseline measurement to show improvement as grace-centered behaviors take root.

Step 5: Reinforce and Repeat
Consistency is essential. Leadership must model grace daily and reinforce desired behaviors:

- Celebrate examples of grace in action.
- Address destructive behaviors promptly, without shaming individuals.
- Review the Grace Grid regularly in meetings to monitor culture and performance.
- Encourage teams to reflect on how they can apply grace in their own roles.

Instructional Tip: Make the Grace Grid a living tool, not a static exercise. Use it to guide decision-making, coaching, and accountability at every level of the organization.

Examples in Action
Retail Example:

- **Indifference:** Cashiers ignore customers, resulting in lower sales.
- **With Grace:** Staff are trained to greet every customer within 30 seconds. Engagement rises, sales increase.

Corporate Example:

- **Assumptions:** New hires are expected to understand processes that were never explained. Projects stall.
- **With Grace:** Standardized onboarding, proactive clarification, and early coaching accelerate performance.Nonprofit Example:

Leadership Challenge

Map your organization on the Grace Grid this week. Identify where your team is standing, where the gaps exist, and where you need to climb.

This exercise allows leaders to see the direct connection between culture, grace, and performance, creating a roadmap for sustainable improvement.

SECTION 6: INTEGRATING GRACE INTO DAILY LEADERSHIP PRACTICES

Understanding grace is one thing. Applying it consistently in daily work is another. This section provides a structured, practical approach to embed grace into your leadership habits and team interactions over time.

The goal is not perfection—it is progressive, intentional improvement. By integrating small, daily actions, grace becomes a habitual part of decision-making, communication, and culture-building.

Week 1: Presence over Indifference
Focus: Show up fully for the people who depend on you.
Daily Actions:
* Day 1: In your next conversation, give your full attention. Put away phones, laptops, and

- distractions. Observe how this affects the interaction.
- Day 2: Send one note of recognition or encouragement to a teammate or direct report. Highlight effort, not just results.
- Day 3: Ask a colleague how they are doing personally, not just professionally. Listen actively.
- Day 4: Block 15 minutes in your calendar to reflect on your team's needs without interruptions.
- Day 5: End the day by writing down one moment where you were fully present and its impact.

Key Insight: Presence is not just being physically available; it is mental and emotional engagement. Small, consistent actions prevent larger issues from taking root.

Week 2: Alignment over Assumptions
Focus: Clarity creates momentum across teams, not just in meetings.
Daily Actions:

- Day 6: Rewrite your team's priorities in a single sentence and share it with someone.
- Day 7: In your next email or meeting, state the purpose first, ensuring everyone understands the "why" before the "what."
- Day 8: Ask one team member: "What's unclear about what we are trying to achieve?" and listen carefully.

- Day 9: Remove or delegate one task that does not align with the larger goal.
- Day 10: Write down the top three priorities for the week and share them openly with your team.

Key Insight: Alignment prevents costly assumptions. Clear communication ensures everyone moves in the same direction.

Week 3: Accountability over Disconnection
Focus: Own what is yours and invite others to do the same.
Daily Actions:

- Day 11: Admit one mistake openly and share what you learned. Model accountability.
- Day 12: Before sending a request, clarify exactly what you expect and by when.
- Day 13: Check in with yourself: Did you follow through on commitments this week?
- Day 14: Thank someone specifically for keeping their word, reinforcing accountability in others.
- Day 15: Ask your team: "What's one thing we can do better next time?" Capture responses and act on them.

Key Insight: Accountability grows from clear expectations and empowered ownership. Teams that practice accountability thrive under pressure.

Week 4: Courage and Ownership over Avoidance and Blame

Focus: Step into spaces others avoid. Lead with honesty, decisiveness, and responsibility.

Daily Actions:

- Day 16: Make one decision you have been postponing and execute it today.
- Day 17: Ask someone for feedback on a recent decision or action. Receive it openly and reflect.
- Day 18: Address one small but nagging issue you have been avoiding. Do not delay.
- Day 19: Speak up once in a situation where you would normally remain silent. Focus on truth and respect.
- Day 20: Invite a team member to lead something you would normally control, modeling ownership and empowerment.

Key Insight: Courage and ownership are learned behaviors. By modeling them daily, you encourage the same in your team.

Week 5: Integration

Focus: Turn daily practices into habitual, cultural behaviors.

Daily Actions:

- Day 21: Revisit your personal top three priorities. Are they aligned with your team's goals and the larger mission?
- Day 22: Ask your team: "Which of the five behaviors are we improving on?" and discuss openly.

- Day 23: Commit to modeling one behavior every week. Track your impact and encourage others to do the same.
- Day 24: Invite each team member to pick one behavior to watch for in themselves and in others.
- Day 25: Celebrate a win—small or large—that came from practicing these habits.

Key Insight: Integration solidifies behavior change. Small, consistent actions over time embed grace into organizational culture, making it self-sustaining.

Closing the Daily Leadership Challenge

- Remember: This is not about perfection. Each day presents opportunities to replace absence with presence, confusion with clarity, excuses with accountability, and fear with courage.
- Focus: Consistency over intensity. Grace becomes visible when leaders model, measure, and reinforce the five behaviors every day.
- Outcome: Teams strengthen, trust grows, performance improves, and organizational resilience is built.

Reflection Question for Leaders:

Which behavior will I focus on this week to model grace most consistently, and how will I measure its impact?

SECTION 7: GRACE-CENTERED HIRING AND TEAM-BUILDING

Building a team with grace at its core is one of the most powerful levers for organizational performance. Leaders often hire for skill alone, overlooking character, emotional intelligence, and cultural fit. Grace-centered hiring goes beyond competence—it identifies people who will strengthen the team, model values, and sustain culture under pressure.

This section provides practical steps and questions to bring grace into every stage of recruiting, onboarding, and team-building.

Step 1: Identify Skills to Prioritize
Grace-driven candidates combine competence with character. Look for:

1. **Adaptive Problem-Solving:** Ability to learn quickly and adjust strategies in real time.
2. **Emotional Intelligence (EQ):** Empathy, self-awareness, and regulation in challenging situations.

3. **Collaborative Leadership:** Can influence without dominating, share credit, and build consensus.
4. **Resilience and Composure:** Maintains calm under pressure, steadiness in uncertainty.
5. **Service Orientation:** Demonstrated history of helping colleagues, clients, or communities succeed.

Instructional Tip: During interviews, dig into past experiences, not just résumés. Ask candidates to describe moments when they had to balance performance with care for others.

Step 2: Examine Work History
Beyond titles and companies, focus on patterns of behavior and cultural impact:

- Patterns of Growth: Did the candidate create lasting impact beyond their job description?
- Ethical Track Record: Look for transparency, integrity, and absence of harmful conduct.
- Cultural Footprints: How did teams perform under their leadership? Were colleagues retained and developed?

Instructional Tip: Ask for examples of challenges overcome, failures learned from, and situations where the candidate had to act with grace under pressure.

Step 3: Assess Communication Styles
Grace shows up in how people speak, listen, and respond under pressure. Look for:

- Clarity + Compassion: Communicates directly but humanely.
- Active Listening: Responds thoughtfully rather than waiting for a turn to speak.
- Conflict Approach: Handles disagreements calmly, constructively, and respectfully.
- Storytelling Ability: Can inspire and influence, not just inform.

Instructional Tip: Include behavioral interview questions that reveal these traits. Observe how candidates interact with staff, peers, and even support personnel during the process.

Step 4: Evaluate Candidate Success Indicators
Traditional metrics (revenue, project completions, sales) matter, but in grace-centered recruiting, ask:
- Did the team they led perform better over time?
- Were relationships preserved or fractured in pursuit of results?
- Did they leave their previous organization healthier than they found it?

Instructional Tip: Look for evidence of sustainable performance paired with empathy and accountability. Candidates who achieve results at the cost of culture may not fit a grace-centered organization.

Step 5: Ask Questions that Surface Grace
Here are practical interview questions to identify candidates who demonstrate grace:

- "Tell me about a time you had to choose between results and relationships. What did you do?"
- "When have you failed, and how did you handle the impact on others?"
- "How do you ensure your team feels seen and heard?"
- "What cause or community outside of work matters most to you, and why?"
- "If I asked three people who disagreed with you about your leadership, what would they say?"

Instructional Tip: Follow up with probing questions. Grace is revealed in nuance, reflection, and consistency over time, not in rehearsed answers.

Step 6: Build Grace-Driven Teams
Grace-driven leaders assemble teams that balance skill, character, and perspective.

- Design for Diversity: Different perspectives create resilience and innovation.
- Practice Inclusion: Ensure quieter voices are drawn in, not drowned out.
- Facilitate Healthy Tension: Turn disagreements into problem-solving rather than division.
- Prioritize Growth: Invest in mentorship, skill development, and succession planning.

Instructional Tip: Teams are more than collections of résumés—they are ecosystems of trust, skill, and collaboration. Consider both who is missing and who is overrepresented when building a team.

Step 7: Seek References That Matter

Not all references are equal. Focus on those who can speak to grace and character:

- Former Direct Reports: Did they feel valued and supported?
- Cross-Functional Peers: Can they provide insight into collaboration and influence?
- Clients or Partners: Observed grace under pressure from an external perspective?
- Supervisors/Boards: Can they attest to transparency, accountability, and long-term impact?

Instructional Tip: Ask references for specific examples of both achievements and failures and how the candidate navigated challenges with integrity and respect.

Step 8: Recognize the Personality Types That Strengthen Teams

Grace-driven teams thrive on balance:

- Visionaries: Inspire risk-taking and see the future.
- Operators: Turn vision into actionable systems.
- Connectors: Build relationships and networks.
- Stabilizers: Keep the team grounded during crises.

Instructional Tip: Avoid over-reliance on any one type. Strength comes from harmony and complementary skills, not uniformity.

THE FIVE BEHAVIORS IN RELATIONSHIPS: A CASE STUDY

The poisons Janis had warned about weren't just threats to performance metrics. They also worked quietly in relationships, shaping how people trusted—or failed to trust—each other. Karen and Janis had lived through all five.

Indifference showed up first in the form of distance. Karen, unsettled by the photo, began to withdraw. Conversations became shorter, more formal, and the warmth of their early connection disappeared. Indifference in relationships doesn't always look like hostility—it often looks like cool silence, a closed door where openness used to be.

Assumptions followed quickly. Karen assumed Janis had dug up the photo to undermine her, while Janis assumed Karen's sudden coldness was rooted in judgment about her diagnosis or her approach to the company. Neither spoke these fears aloud, but both carried them quietly, letting suspicion widen the gap.

Disconnection set in next. What had begun with friendly lunches and shared ideas narrowed into perfunctory check-ins. Janis noticed the missing eye contact, the clipped tone. Karen noticed how guarded Janis had become in her responses. Both women felt it, but neither broke the silence.

Avoidance took root as the unspoken stretched on. The hard conversation—the one that could have cleared the air—was postponed. Each encounter danced around what mattered most, choosing professionalism over honesty. Avoidance preserved order, but at the cost of trust.

And finally, **blame**—the quietest but sharpest of them all. Karen blamed Janis in her thoughts for the stress she felt at work and at home, even though Janis had never raised the issue herself. For a time, that unspoken blame poisoned the ground between them.

But just as these poisons had been named and confronted in the store, they were dismantled between the two women.

Care replaced indifference when Karen finally admitted the truth of her fears.

Clarity replaced assumptions when she forgave Janis and owned her part.

Connection replaced disconnection as their smiles turned genuine again.

Action replaced avoidance as Karen chose honesty over distance.

And **shared responsibility** replaced blame as both women agreed to move forward together.

The same transformation that brought life back to the store also breathed life back into a fragile relationship. Metrics could be measured on a spreadsheet. Relationships couldn't. But in the end, the evidence was no less visible—in trust rebuilt, in warmth restored, in two leaders choosing grace over suspicion.

AN IMPORTANT OBSERVATION

As Janis visited stores across each region, one pattern became impossible to ignore. The winning stores talked about winning—every day. Success wasn't just an occasional goal; it was woven into their language, their conversations, their culture. The team members knew what they were aiming for, celebrated small victories, and kept their eyes on the prize.

But in the losing stores, talk of winning was rare—sometimes completely absent. In fact, many teams didn't even realize they were losing. They lacked awareness of how they were performing, what the numbers meant, or how far behind they had fallen.

One of the biggest reasons became clear when Janis looked for the metrics that track performance. In the winning stores, key numbers were posted prominently—right where every employee could see them, in break rooms or near workstations. Those stores had clear scoreboards that kept everyone accountable and motivated.

In contrast, losing stores had no such visibility. Sometimes, the metrics existed but were hidden away in the manager's office or locked in reports no one else saw. Without a visible scoreboard, the team had no real way to measure progress or react in real time. There was no sense of urgency, no collective push for victory, no reason to fight harder.

The absence of a scoreboard in a business is no different from removing it from a football stadium. Imagine a game where no one in the stands knows the score until the final whistle blows. The fans wouldn't know when to cheer or when to rally the team. Their gratitude for effort would be muted because they couldn't see the stakes. The celebrations would come too late—if they came at all. Engagement would vanish.

The same thing happens in an organization without a scoreboard. Teams wander through the "game" without knowing whether they're ahead or behind. Effort becomes inconsistent, unpredictable—more about surviving the day than striving for victory. Leaders assume their people understand the numbers, but without visibility, most don't. The scoreboard is what tells them not just if they're winning, but how to win —what small moves matter, what adjustments shift the momentum, what actions compound into breakthroughs.

Janis also noticed another critical piece: in the best stores, leaders used the scoreboard as part of their daily rhythm. They didn't just hang the numbers on the wall—they talked about them in morning huddles, asked their teams what they meant, and celebrated when progress showed. These conversations sharpened focus. They reminded everyone that doing the little things right—stocking shelves on time, greeting customers warmly, keeping displays fresh—was what ultimately moved the needle on the big things, like sales and customer loyalty.

She remembered walking into one of those winning stores early one morning. The team had gathered in the break room, standing around a simple whiteboard that listed yesterday's sales, today's goal, and the number of loyalty sign-ups they needed to stay on pace. The manager didn't give a lecture. Instead, she asked the team: "What's the score? Where do we stand?" The employees answered in unison, and then each shared one action they could take to help hit the day's target. The entire exchange took less than five minutes, but the energy in the room was undeniable. People walked out smiling, shoulders squared, ready to work.

Contrast that with the losing stores, where Janis often found employees starting their shifts in silence, unaware of yesterday's results or today's expectations. With no scoreboard, they were like athletes stumbling onto the field without knowing the rules, the score, or even which direction to run.

And then there was the coaching—or rather, the lack of it. In many struggling stores, the coaches were missing in action. They weren't leading, encouraging, or guiding their teams to improve. Without coaching, the scoreboard was silent even if it existed—the players had no one to help them interpret it or use it to adjust strategy. Winning stores had leaders who acted like great coaches: present on the field, engaged with the play, translating numbers into action.

But perhaps the strangest and most telling discovery was that the customers knew. They could tell the store was losing before anyone on the team did. It showed in the dirt left on the floors, the tired and distracted expressions on employees' faces, the cluttered and disorganized shelves, and price tags that didn't match the ads. Many customers only shopped there because the alternative stores were too far away, not because they wanted to.

Janis realized that when a store is winning, customers feel it—they become part of the energy and the joy. But when a store loses, the loss extends beyond the team. The customers lose too.

And this is where grace matters. Grace doesn't mean lowering expectations or looking the other way when performance slips. It means creating an environment where employees can win—at work and at home. It extends to holding people accountable in ways that encourage them to be their best selves. Grace is the leader who posts the scoreboard not to shame the team, but to give them a clear path to improvement. It's the coach who insists on daily check-ins, not as busywork, but as a way to keep people engaged, purposeful, and hopeful.

Grace helps employees discover more joy in their work because it connects effort with meaning. It gives them a tangible reason to do better for themselves, their teams, and their families. And when grace is present, winning isn't just about hitting numbers—it's about building people who carry that sense of purpose beyond the workplace into every corner of their lives. Because in the end, a scoreboard shows the score—but grace makes sure people never forget why the game is worth playing.

ACKNOWLEDGEMENTS

To my friends—I am deeply and sincerely grateful for each of you. Your love, encouragement, and unwavering belief in me fueled my inspiration at every stage of this journey. I could not have written this book without the light you've brought into my life.

To my family—thank you for granting me the quiet space I needed to think, dream, and write. You made countless sacrifices, giving so much of yourselves so I could fully immerse in the ideas that fill these pages. For that, I am eternally thankful.

To everyone who shaped the look and feel of this book—your guidance, creative insights, and generous feedback elevated this work beyond what I could have imagined. I hope reading it has been as meaningful for you as your contributions have been for me.

To my readers—you are the reason this book exists. Your time, attention, and willingness to engage with these words allow me to reach hearts and minds all over the world. I promise to carry the love I receive from you and pass it on to those who need it most.

To the leaders who shaped my path—thank you for challenging me, stretching me, and teaching me that leadership is about more than titles—it's about character. Pete Renkes, your encouragement to step into management changed the course of my life. Your belief in me leaves me forever grateful.

To the sales professionals who tested and pushed me—you demanded more of me than I thought I had to give, and in doing so, you accelerated my growth in ways I'll never forget. Without those challenges, this book would not have been possible.

And to the love of my life—nothing here, and nothing in my life's work, would be possible without you. Your steady support, unshakable encouragement, and willingness to embrace the demands of my writing made this journey lighter and brighter. I love you, always and forever.

In the end, this book is not just mine—it belongs to everyone who believed in me, stood by me, and gave me the courage to finish what I started.

ABOUT THE AUTHOR

Calvin D. Morris brings a rare blend of strategic insight and creative passion. With executive leadership in retail operations—including managing multi-market stores and spearheading logistics teams—Calvin learned firsthand how leadership decisions shape performance, culture, and growth. He channels those insights into his creative work.

Calvin is the founder of the audio production site ESP by SNJ and the author of two books: Escaping Poverty: The Four Categories and Pages of Life. Born in the South and now based in the Midwest, he infuses his regional experiences into writing, podcasting, music, and web design—where creativity meets strategy.

He is also the founder of Disc Golf Core Unit, a blog and brand dedicated to disc golf culture, apparel, and community connection. Whether he's producing audio, building brands, or writing his next book, Calvin's goal remains the same: to create work that informs, inspires, and leaves a lasting impact.

AUTHOR'S NOTES

In my career, I've worked in some very challenging cultures. Many of the environments I stepped into were already struggling, and often I didn't have a choice about where I went—I was simply sent where the need was greatest. That meant inheriting low-performing stores, difficult teams, and circumstances that would have discouraged many.

But I never saw those assignments as punishment. I saw them as opportunity. Opportunity to test myself, to find ways to turn performance around, and to leave something better than I found it. In those moments, I discovered some of the same truths Janis uncovers in this book: that behind every failing metric is a human story, and behind every struggling team is potential waiting to be unlocked.

Like Janis, I wanted to impact the lives of my people—not just in their professional roles, but in their personal lives as well. That meant giving more than the bare minimum. I poured energy into training sessions, role-playing exercises, coaching conversations, and encouragement. I invested in their growth because I believed they could rise higher than they imagined.

Early on, I also learned something crucial: a leader must take charge of the environment right away. The atmosphere of a workplace doesn't just "happen"—it's created. I remember walking into one store where the culture was heavy with negativity. Customers could feel it the moment they stepped inside. So, from day one, I made it a point to greet employees with energy, celebrate small wins out loud, and share daily reminders of gratitude. Before long, the team started smiling more, laughing more, and bringing that same energy to the customers. Sales followed.

At the same time, leaders can never forget that employees bring their full lives with them into the workplace. They're not just workers—they're people navigating marriage, divorce, children, bills, financial stress, and countless unseen burdens. I'll never forget one team member who confided in me that she was on the edge of quitting—not because of the job itself, but because of challenges at home. Instead of writing her off, I worked with her schedule, encouraged her, and gave her space to regroup. She not only stayed, but she eventually became one of the strongest leaders in the district.

And that's where grace came in for me. Leading with grace didn't mean lowering standards. Quite the opposite. Grace allowed me to hold my teams accountable while still respecting their dignity. It allowed me to push for results without crushing creativity. Grace gave me a way to say, I believe in you enough to expect more from you.

This book is born from those years, those teams, and those lessons. It's a reflection of what I saw, what I lived, and what I believe: that grace is the greatest strength a leader can have. Grace creates space for people to grow, and when people grow, organizations flourish.

If there's one thing I hope you carry from these pages into your own leadership, it's this: results matter, but people matter more. Lead with both in mind. Lead with grace.

GRACE

THE MOST UNDERUTILIZED
STRENGTH IN BUSINESS

THE END

www.ingramcontent.com/pod-product-compliance
Lightning Source LLC
Chambersburg PA
CBHW071555210326
41597CB00019B/3261